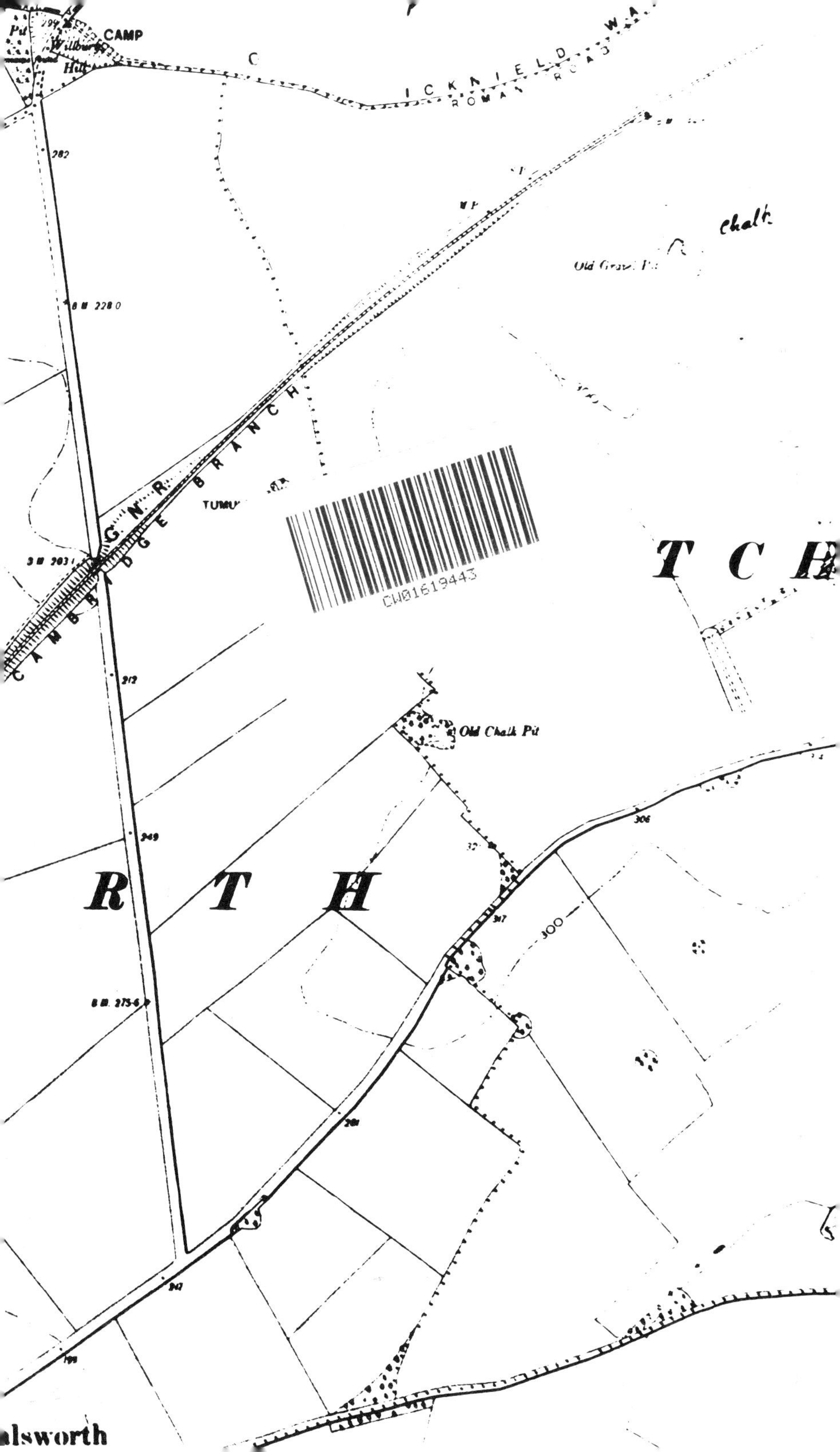
CAMP
Pit
Hill
ICKNIELD WA
ROMAN ROAD
282
Old Gravel Pit
Chalk
G N R
CAMBRIDGE BRANCH
TUMU
T C H
Old Chalk Pit
212
306
249
R T H
300
alsworth

TO HAVE
AND TO HOLD

An Account
of Frederick Bandet's Life
in Business

By the Same Author

COMPANY HISTORIES:

Men and Machines: D. Napier & Son 1808-1958
(with C.H. Wilson)
Hard Roads and Highways: SPD Limited 1918-1968
The Weir Group: a Centenary History
Imperial Chemical Industries: a History
Vol. 1 *The Forerunners, 1870-1926*
Vol. 2 *The First Quarter-Century, 1926-1952*
Metal Box: A History
A House in the City
Fifty Years of Unilever

BIOGRAPHY:

Architect of Air Power: the Life of the first Viscount Weir, 1877-1959

GENERAL HISTORY:

Life in Victorian England (reissued as *Victorian England)*
Professional Men: the Rise of the Professional Classes in Nineteenth-Century England
The Middle Classes
Macadam: the McAdam Family and the Turnpike Roads

Photograph by Lichfield 1983

Frederick Bandet

TO HAVE AND TO HOLD

An Account of Frederick Bandet's Life in Business

By W. J. Reader

Endpapers:
(Front) Extract from the 1949 Ordnance Survey showing the site of the Hitchin Industrial Estate and surrounding. Scale 6 inches to 1 mile.

(Rear) Extract from the 1960 Ordnance Survey showing the development of the same area. Scale 6 inches to one mile.

ISBN 0-95089-520 2

Designed by Richard Downer FSIAD FSTD
President, Society of Typographic Designers

Printed by Lund Humphries, Bradford.

Set in Baskerville 11 point leaded 2 points

Author's Acknowledgements

My account of the career of Dr. Frederick Bandet is chiefly founded on interviews with:
Mr. Cecil Baker; Dr. Frederick Bandet, his daughters Gina and Isabel, his son Henry, and his sister Mrs E. Barker; Mr. B. Bates; Mrs Joyce Cannings; Mr. Alfred A. Davies; Mr. D.F. Desmond; Mr. A.J. Edmonds; Mr. K.D.F. Guyton; Mr. F. Hillyard; Mr. J. Hill; Mr. E. Howlett; the late Mr. A. King; Mr. D.B. Moore; Mr. D.W. Morgan; Mr. J.P. Raisman; Mr. P. Smyth; Mr. J. Vivian; Mrs B. Wearmouth.

I should like to thank all those who were kind enough to talk to me, and to make it clear that for the use made of the material they provided I alone am responsible.

I should also like to record my thanks to members of the staff of Hunting Gate Group at Hitchin and in California, and especially to Mr. Peter Sanctuary for his help with the illustrations and to Mr. J.R. Cowen for help and advice at every stage of the book's preparation. Miss Susan Cowen prepared the typescript.

June 1983 W.J.R.

Contents

Illustrations

Foreword

THIS book is a story of enterprise and initiative, of the success that crowned the efforts of a man who, with very little in the way of capital resources, arrived alone in this country barely able to speak the language. Like others seeking refuge here from persecution or poverty he not only survived but prospered. His is a story of thrift and caution, of determination and the application of sound judgement, culminating in a substantial business benefiting not merely himself and his family but the employees and the community as well.

The Directors of Hunting Gate had three objectives in deciding to publish this book.

First, we recognised that it was not unique. Over the years there have been thousands of similar examples and, indeed, small businesses and the people who built them are, and always have been, fundamental to the strength of Great Britain. Not many, perhaps too few, of these stories are known and we felt that if the one about our own Company set an example and gave hope and ideas to even a small number of able young people now starting out on their careers it would be worthwhile.

Secondly we wished our own staff to learn, through the pen of a leading corporate historian, not just how their Company came into being but also to draw, from the experience of the past, lessons for the future. The importance of being a caring employer; of employing the best people and knowing how to motivate them; of being wary of speculation; of prudence in accounting and valuation policies; of pioneering new business practices; of maintaining sound financial control; and above all of establishing capable mangement succession. These are the lessons to be found in this book. We believe they are as valid and as relevant today as they were a quarter of a century ago.

Finally, this book is our tribute to the man about whom it is written: Frederick Bandet, our Founder, in this his seventieth year. For nearly 25 years FB was Chairman and Managing Director of Hunting Gate and the Investment Companies which he created and expanded into profitable growth. We are proud to publish his example of skilful and determined effort. FB recruited, trained and groomed the management team that was to succeed him when, in 1976, for reasons which will become clear to the reader, he moved to California. Not to retire but to take on a challenge that might well daunt a much younger man: to start afresh, once again in a strange land. Once again he has been successful.

FB remains the conscientious proprietor, concerned about the welfare of his staff, interested in the care of his assets and the steady expansion of his companies, able and willing to give guidance and advice whenever it is asked for.

FB sought and received in this country the shelter and protection he needed at a critical time in his life. He has provided many good jobs and has added to our national stock of offices and factories. His story may inspire young men today to follow his example.

C.J. Baker
Chairman
Hunting Gate Group

June 1983

Chapter One

GROUP PORTRAIT HUNTING GATE IN 1982

Group Portrait-Hunting Gate in 1982

LAND is the oldest source of wealth; the most permanent source of wealth; perhaps in the end the only real source of wealth, for without land what wealth is possible? Certainly the lawyers once took this view; hence the terms 'real property' and 'real estate'. But land by itself is a source of wealth, not wealth itself. If wealth is to be created from it, something must be done with it. Capital must be invested in it, risks must be taken with it, skills of many kinds must be employed on it. It must be 'developed'.

To succeed, the property developer needs shrewd commercial judgement, including an indefinable 'nose' for opportunities. He also needs a broad appreciation of what is going on around him, giving him an instructed view of the likely future and the self-confidence to act upon it. To the extent that he has these qualities, his success will be of his own making, but he is very vulnerable to circumstances beyond his own control. Even more than most business men, the property developer needs a generally hopeful and expansive economic environment; unless things are going pretty well for people in general he can hardly hope to prosper.

For many centuries landowners–and others–have been well aware of the opportunities of their day, whether they were Cistercian abbots running sheep on unfarmable land in the 13th century, 'new men' eager for monastic lands in Henry VIII's time, or Georgian gentry in pursuit of enclosure acts to improve their estates. Property development in England, and no doubt in other countries too, is an ancient and respectable occupation.

Nowhere has this been more true, over the last two or three centuries, than in London, for London over much of that time has answered more or less to the enthusiastic description in the

Report of the 1871 Census:
'The metropolis of the Empire stands . . . by itself; it is the seat of the Legislature, the primary Home of Justice, Medicine and Religion, the theatre for the fine arts and the sciences, the great centre of society; the emporium of commerce, the warehouse of England, the great Port in communication with the sea. Spanning the broad tidal waters of the embanked Thames with its magnificent bridges, it wants but a greater number of grand public buildings to be the first Queen of Cities.'

Put more coarsely, if you owned land in London and were far-sighted in what you did with it, you could hardly fail to do well.

Some such thought must have been in the mind of Sir Thomas Grosvenor when in 1676, at the age of twenty, he came up to London and married Mary Davies, aged eleven, heiress of Alexander Davies, a scrivener, who had died in 1665. Grosvenor's family, says the *Dictionary of National Biography*, 'was of great antiquity in Cheshire, but of moderate fortune.' Mary Davies' marriage portion included a large sum in cash 'and a considerable estate, known as Ebury Farm, "towards Chelsea", over which Belgrave Square and Pimlico now extend, and another large holding between Tyburn Brook and Park Lane, on part of which Grosvenor Square was afterwards built.'

The Grosvenors were not alone among land-owning families in being shrewd enough and bold enough to seize their opportunities. With the professional help of surveyors, architects, lawyers and building contractors the Grosvenors, the Berkeleys, the Russells, the Portmans, the Cavendishes and other proprietors laid out the streets, squares and terraces of Belgravia, Mayfair, Bloomsbury and the Regent's Park district where the Park itself, the Nash terraces and Regent Street demonstrate the breadth of the Prince Regent's vision.

For an aspiring property developer, the ownership of land was not necessary – though it helped. Thomas Cubitt (1788-

1855) began as a journeyman carpenter and then, like carpenters before and since his time, became a builder. To keep his men employed he began 'to take ground for building', says the *Dictionary of National Biography*, 'a species of speculation, which afterwards became the employment of his life.' About 1824, on land leased from the Duke of Bedford – the pattern of activity is still familiar today – he put up a good deal of Bloomsbury. Then, aware how fashionable the western suburbs were becoming, he moved westward. South Belgravia is his monument.

Many builders, in a much smaller way, tried to do the same as Thomas Cubitt. Some succeeded; many, perhaps most, failed. Their careers all illustrate the opportunities and the risks open both to builders and to those whose professional training as architects, lawyers, surveyors, land agents and others, fitted them in one way or another, if they were bold enough, to go in for property development – not in the service of landowners but on their own account.

Alert developers in the 19th century, in London and throughout the country, were quick to notice a commercial opportunity, to recognise the implications of technical progress, to detect a social trend that could be turned to their advantage, and their works are all around us still. The sixth Duke of Bedford rebuilt Covent Garden market in 1830. The Marquess of Bute, much later in the century, developed Cardiff as the Welsh coal trade boomed. Various landowners, recognising that more and more people could afford to go on holiday by train, co-operated with railway companies in turning obscure fishing villages, which they happened to own, into flourishing seaside resorts. The Dukes of Devonshire, following this principle, transformed Eastbourne. The Dukes of Devonshire also owned Buxton, the Derbyshire spa, and did the same kind of thing there. 'The great landlords of England', wrote T.H.S. Escott in 1878, 'are really the rulers of principalities . . . They are charged with the administration of a miniature empire, which often embraces a number of provinces, whose conditions, resources, and necessities differ as much as if they were separate kingdoms.' In making the most of their resources, the great landowners were enthusiastically, and sometimes successfully, imitated by a host of lesser developers, who owned no land at all, or very little, but had ideas on how land could be put to use and were prepared to risk putting their ideas into practice on their own. The closest modern parallel is probably the activities of certain great property developers: Sir John Laing, Lord Taylor and others.

The Hunting Gate Group is concerned with all aspects of the ownership, development, letting and sale of industrial, commercial and house property. About the only major branch of the property business which it does not touch is agricultural land. It is organised to carry a project from the first recognition of an opportunity and the acquisition of a site, through the construction phase, to the sale or letting of the completed buildings and, if necessary, to the management of the property after it has been let.

As a many-sided property enterprise, Hunting Gate has something in common with the great estates so grandiloquently described by Escott. Its prosperity, like theirs, depends on the profitable use of land. Those who run the Group's affairs, like the great landowners, need shrewd commercial sense, sound financial planning, and the support of professional and technical services. Finally, in the Group as in the estates, the influence of the founder and his family is continuous and strong.

Grosvenor Square 1754, from Stow's Survey.
Hunting Gate opened its London office in Grosvenor Street on 1st September 1981.

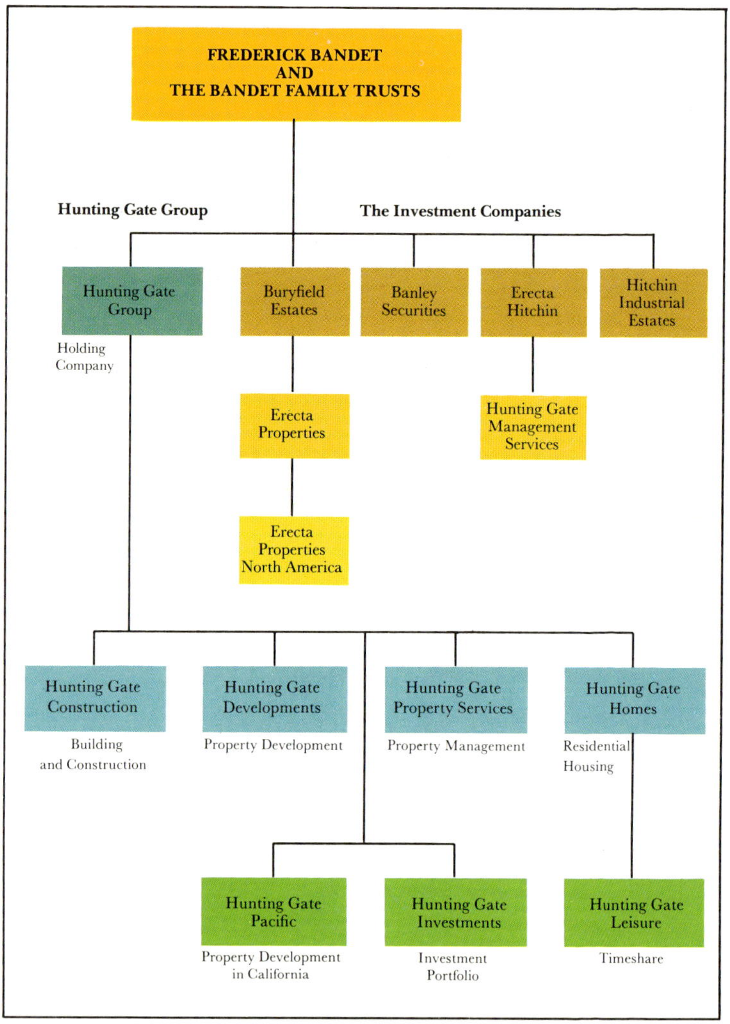

The corporate structure

The founder of a great estate is likely to lie under brass or marble in a country church, like Robert Cecil at Hatfield. Not so the founder of Hunting Gate. He is Frederick Bandet, living today in California though he was born a subject of the Austrian Emperor in 1913. Just after the end of the Second World War, he set up in business, in a very small way, in the ancient Hertfordshire town of Hitchin. From that beginning the present Group has grown. Today it is active both in this country and in California, and its assets are counted in tens of millions of pounds.

Why Hitchin?

Why 'Hunting Gate'?

Why California?

These and all sorts of other questions arise. To find the answers let us start by looking at the Group as it stands at the present day, and then go back to its origins.

The property developer's essential raw materials are land and money. Of the two in Great Britain, land is much the scarcer. There is not much of it, and about half of what there is cannot be used except for grouse-shooting, hill-walking, deer-stalking, rock-climbing, bird-watching and other healthy outdoor pastimes, with perhaps a few sheep to give animation to the landscape. Of the land which is usable, a great deal is not available for development because it is needed for farming.

The developers are, therefore, in competition with each other for a much sought-after commodity; the more so because the location of a piece of land is critical to its desirability. Houses must be put where people are likely to want to live; shops, offices, factories, and warehouses where potential tenants can

Hunting Gate's Head Office in Hitchin, Hertfordshire.

see advantage for their business. Persuasion, advertising and publicity can be brought to bear with greater or less effect, local authorities and the Government can offer inducements; but in the end matters will be decided by the facts of economic geography, particularly communications and labour supply for manufacturing industry and, for private housing, accessibility or otherwise to employment, to schools, to shops and to the things that make life pleasant, varying from hunting in the Cotswolds to theatres and concert halls in London, and a golf club round the corner in a prosperous suburb.

Money, in contrast to land, even in the depths of the worst recession for fifty years, is not scarce. On the contrary, it is almost embarrassingly plentiful, thanks mainly to the growth over the last thirty years or so of the great pension funds and insurance companies, and the direction which their investment policy has taken in times of rapidly rising inflation. As pension contributions and insurance premiums flow in, so funds for investment must flow out without too much delay and, as a store of value, well-chosen property, let to well-chosen tenants, has no equal. 'Safe as houses', our ancestors used to say, and the great landowners followed that principle, not necessarily confining it to houses. There are always very large sums of money seeking a home, provided the conditions hinted at above, with their emphasis on 'well-chosen', are met.

That is the industrial and commercial aspect of property development, taking physical shape in offices, factories, warehouses and shops, built to be bought by the institutions or by investment companies such as those managed by the Hunting Gate Group though not owned by it. There is also a different class of property-owner or would-be owner: the private individual. In England and the USA, far less so on the

Continent, the urge to own the house or flat one lives in is very strong, and the taxation system encourages it by treating house purchase, for the buyer's occupation, as a privileged kind of investment. Whether this is wise or not is debatable, but at least it means that there are always people hoping to borrow money on mortgage, thus providing another outlet for big institutional lenders: in this case the insurance companies and the building societies and, recently, the banks in competition with them. For Hunting Gate, and other house-builders, it means that if they can find the right places to build the right kind of houses – and judgements of what is 'right' are not easy to make – they can usually expect to sell them.

Here then is the central activity of the property developer: to put together a product – land and the buildings on it – that can be profitably let or sold. Property developers come in many shapes and sizes. Some are individuals who simply buy and sell pieces of land, with or without buildings, perhaps as a spare time occupation. There are entrepreneurs with West End offices, a small secretarial staff, and little more. At times they will employ architects and builders to improve existing property, to rebuild or build afresh, but they are not builders themselves. They are armchair developers. What all these individuals have in common is the search for a cash transaction, the search for immediate profit.

Hunting Gate is in a different class, the class of builder-developers, in a more or less direct line of succession from Thomas Cubitt, taking the closest interest in every stage of a project and seeking to create lasting assets rather than quick profits. The Group manufactures buildings, and as with other manufacturers marketing is as important as production, for the cost of holding unsold buildings on borrowed money quickly becomes ruinous. Tenants must be found for commercial and industrial property, buyers for houses, with the utmost urgency.

Within the Hunting Gate Group the major responsibility for creating new developments, especially on the industrial, commercial and retail side, lies, according to the organisation chart, with Hunting Gate Developments Limited which is headed by Jonathan Walters ARICS. Charts, however, are well known for displaying the form rather than the spirit of an organisation and, since all the Group's four senior executives serve on the Development Company's Board, they are all to be regarded, and regard themselves, as sharing the responsibility, alongside their other responsibilities, of seeking new business. New business cannot be passively awaited. It must be actively sought through close personal contact, in and out of office hours, with a wide range of the leading London and provincial firms of chartered surveyors.

Without personal respect, personal confidence, personal trust, without an untarnished record as a reliable and punctual builder, opportunities would not flow towards Hunting Gate, nor would the pension funds and insurance companies be persuaded to put up money, nor would banks extend credit over the years as they have done, in good times and bad. It was on such a basis of personal credit that Frederick Bandet built the financial foundations on which the present Group was established. Among his greatest services to the Group was creating, before the Group itself was formed, the nucleus of a full-time, largely professional 'in-house' team capable of building the confidence which the Group now inspires. It has provided Hunting Gate with an asset which the casual reader of the balance sheet may not fully recognise, but which those who matter in the property business recognise very clearly indeed.

When a developer identifies an opportunity, his work begins. He must seek potential investors and tenants, apply for planning permission, contend with opposition – which there is almost certain to be, if the project is on any but the smallest scale – and then, assuming that the work is to go ahead, see to financing it, to acquiring the site, to arranging building work, to leasing or selling the finished product.

There is work here for surveyors, architects, accountants, lawyers, civil and structural engineers, building technologists, to name only some of the more obvious occupations. How is the developer to deal with these matters? One answer is to employ the lowest possible number of people himself and buy advice and services outside, which keeps the developer's fixed costs low and gives him a large range of specialists to choose from. On the other hand, he has little control over them. He has to take his turn with other clients, and he cannot count on punctuality.

Hunting Gate's answer, in common with a few other developers, is to employ professionally and technically qualified people directly and thus provide a wide range of services for the Group itself and for its clients. This way of doing things has its dangers. Good specialists are not cheap to employ and, if there is not enough work for them, costs may rise alarmingly. Empire-building is a temptation not always resisted, and there is far less flexibility in the numbers of people employed, if they are directly on the firm's pay roll, than if they are employed free-lance, on contract, or as employees of outside firms. Moreover, in the case of professional advisers, there is a niggling, uneasy feeling abroad that professional advice *ought* to come from independent practitioners, but that problem is not peculiar to property development: it is endemic in modern business.

BOC's 123,000 sq. ft. offices, factory and social facilities at Ramsgate, 1977.

Hunting Gate Homes' headquarters in Park Street, Hitchin.

On the other side of the account, the considerable advantages of 'in-house' services are evident. They can be deployed exclusively for the benefit of the Group and its clients without regard to any other outside party whatsoever, and the saving of time may be dramatic. Such matters as technical design, style, quality, time-keeping are within the Group's control, so that a complete 'Design and Build' service can confidently be offered.

The Group has been in the housing business, as later chapters will show, since 1964. The subsidiary which looks after it, and of which Ken Price is the Managing Director, is called Hunting Gate Homes Limited, following the unfortunate American usage which blunts the edge of the English language by confusing 'homes' with 'houses'. From its offices in Hitchin, housed in the same new, carefully Georgian building which also contains its own Housing Advisory Centre, the company co-ordinates the activities of its own site-finders, planners, architects and building surveyors. All are closely allied to a specialised sales and marketing organisation so that the entire process of providing houses, from the acquisition of sites, through designing and building, to the final transactions with the buyers, including finance if they need it, can either be handled within the Hunting Gate Group or placed outside if that is more convenient.

In 1983 the Group expects to make more than £1¼ million profit from building several hundred houses, chiefly within its home territory stretching twenty or thirty miles round Hitchin, but with outliers further afield, especially on the outskirts of London – Borehamwood, Northwood, Chessington. Some will be quite large, with four bedrooms and double garages, but in recent years, times being as they are, a policy has been

A two-bedroom starter house, Kings Langley.

developed of building very small houses with a single bedroom, or perhaps two, for people buying for the first time. With building land in North Hertfordshire costing at present around £200,000 per acre, prices can hardly be low, but it may be possible to get prices for these small houses, within forty miles of London, down from £21,000 - £22,000 to about £15,000.

For people who already have a house, and money to spare, 'time-sharing' may have advantages: that is, buying the lease of a holiday house, bungalow or flat for the same period during each year, with the right to sub-let in any year when the leaseholder doesn't want to use it himself. This is one of the leisure industries which are widely expected to grow rapidly during the eighties, and time-sharing itself has been growing for some years in the United Kingdom and abroad. It attracted Hunting Gate's attention in 1980 because it seemed near enough to building and property development to be undertaken confidently, yet far enough removed from the Group's existing activities to provide a welcome opportunity for spreading the Group's risks.

Hunting Gate Leisure Limited was therefore set up to go into time-sharing, under the alluring slogan 'Peace for Sale', at Blakeney in North Norfolk. It offers eighty-year time-sharing leases in properties ranging from houses where eight people can sleep comfortably down to bungalows and flats for two, and behind their double-glazing they are lavishly furnished and equipped with colour television, video recorders and a range of kitchen and laundry machines which might be expected to content most people, though one buyer has complained of the lack of an ice-crusher! Prices range from £1,600 at the low end to £4,825 at the top, giving the right to a week's use of the property every year, and varying according to the

'Fishermens' Cottages' built in 1981 for Hunting Gate Leisure at Blakeney, Norfolk, and let on 80-year timeshare leases.

An example of the standard of quality. This kitchen is equipped with dishwasher, washing machine, extractor fan, eye-level double oven, built-in microwave oven and built-in fridge/freezer.

type of property and the season of the year chosen. As well as the right to sub-let, each new lessee gets a year's subscription to an organisation called Resorts Condominiums International, which enables him to exchange with other time-sharers in many other parts of the world. The venture is new; how it will develop remains to be seen, but over the last few years the popularity of time-sharing has been growing and if you want to watch birds, walk, sail (all the Hunting Gate Leisure leases carry with them the use of a boat) or simply to have some peace, Blakeney is an attractive place.

If buildings, speaking in manufacturing terms, are the property developer's marketable product, then the building industry must be important to him; yet not all developers take an active part in it themselves – they rely on contractors. That was not Bandet's way from the very first. He was not brought up to building (he was educated as a lawyer) but building fascinated him and, as a natural consequence, Hunting Gate is active in the building industry through Hunting Gate Construction Limited, whose Managing Director is Martin Hemmings MCIOB. The Construction Company's boards appear on building sites, chiefly industrial or commercial, as far from Hitchin as Glasgow, although the greater part of the company's work is in the South East and the South Midlands. On these sites the work of the Group's commercial, financial, technical and professional staff takes material form in bricks and mortar or whatever constructional materials may be appropriate. More than a million square feet of industrial and commercial premises were in hand in 1982 and the Construction Company's turnover for 1983 is expected to approach £20 million.

4444 Hunting Gate

The Hunting Gate Group, like other leading firms in the same line of business – notably Wates–is a private company. Nearly 70% of the capital is held by Frederick Bandet and his family trusts. The remainder is in the hands of four executive directors – Danny Desmond, Eric Howlett, David Morgan and Nigel Turnbull and a few senior and long serving members of the staff.

Howlett joined Hunting Gate in 1966, Desmond in 1968, Morgan in 1971 and Turnbull in 1982. They will engage our attention in greater detail later. Here it is sufficient to remark that for more than ten years three of them have shared in direct-

Left to right:
Eric Howlett, Nigel Turnbull, Danny Desmond, David Morgan.

The Hunting Gate Group Board of Directors in session in August 1982.
Left: D.F. Desmond, N.J.C. Turnbull, E. Howlett, J.R. Cowen, K.D.F. Guyton, F. Bandet.
Right: H. Bandet, Isabel Bandet, C.J. Baker (Chairman), A.J. Edmonds, H.E.M. Barnes.

ing the operations of a group of companies in which the value of the assets has risen many times over and whose profits have increased year by year until, in 1982, they were over ten times greater than they were in 1972. Few Boards in the country in this gloomy period, even after allowing for the effects of inflation, can have seen such results from their policies.

Frederick Bandet himself, the founder of the Group, holds non-executive office as a director and as President. For many years, even before the point was taken by the Governor of the Bank of England in a lecture to the Institute of Directors in November 1978, Bandet has recognised the importance of non-executive directors in a private company. The Chairman of Hunting Gate Group is Cecil Baker FIA, well-known in the property business as Chairman of the Property Unit Trust Group, the Alliance Building Society and the Victory Insurance Co. (a subsidiary of Legal & General), and as a Director of

Abbey Life.

Baker is supported by his predecessor in the Chair, Keith Guyton, a Chartered Accountant who has known Bandet since his earliest days in England; by Michael Barnes, also a Chartered Accountant previously in practice in the City, and by John Cowen. Cowen is a business man of wide experience who came on the Hunting Gate Board in 1981 in circumstances to be examined in Chapter Eight.

The birthplace of the Hunting Gate enterprise, in the late 1940's, was the Hitchin Industrial Estate, on the Northern edge of the town. Here the Group still has its head office, in a road called Hunting Gate because it points towards the site of a gate alleged to have been used, in times gone by, for riding to hounds. In the Industrial Estate, Frederick Bandet has a great deal of capital invested, since for many years his policy was not to sell property but to lease it, retaining the ownership through investment companies set up for the benefit of himself and, through trusts, of his family. These companies, with the passage of time and the growth of the business, have come to own property well beyond Hitchin, but the Industrial Estate is still very important to them and to Bandet himself, emotionally as well as financially, for it gave him the chance of his earliest success.

The Investment Companies, except for one in which a Hunting Gate Director has an interest, are wholly owned by Bandet and it is through them that the bulk of the family fortune is held. The Hunting Gate Group itself holds no part of their capital but their properties are managed, along with others belonging

Hitchin Industrial Estate, looking North, 1980.

to the Group itself, by Hunting Gate Property Services Limited which is headed by Michael Rickards ARICS. The Investment Companies contribute importantly to the Group's prosperity. First, they are potential buyers of property which the Group offers for sale. Secondly, it sometimes suits tenants of the Investment Companies to bid for factories which the Group has built or intends to build. Thirdly, and perhaps most importantly, Hunting Gate Property Services manages the Investment Companies' properties for a fee which is a percentage of their rent roll, and that rent roll is large and growing larger, providing the Group with a reliable and steadily increasing source of income.

In 1976 Frederick Bandet went to live in California but not, as might have been expected at his age – then 62 – to retire.

An office development in Spur Road, Orpington, owned by Erecta Properties, one of the Investment Companies, and built by Hunting Gate, 1982.

He intended to go in for property development as he had gone in for it in England some thirty years earlier. He ceased for some years to be a director of the Hunting Gate Group and of the Investment Companies, but he was very far indeed from losing touch. He says himself that his telephone bill has always been large, but it must have grown very much larger after his move to California, for scarcely a day would pass without at least one call, usually at about five in the afternoon (London time), to one or other of the Group directors.

The Californian business, like the business in England, has two main aspects: an investment management company – Hunting Gate Management Company Inc. – wholly owned by Bandet, for whom it is building up a property portfolio; and a subsidiary of the Hunting Gate Group, Hunting Gate Pacific Limited. The activities of both companies are concentrated on San Francisco and its immediate neighbourhood, and on "Silicon Valley", some thirty miles or so to the South, where the

Orinda Towers, Contra Costa County, California; an office development by Hunting Gate Pacific, 1981.

silicon chip was developed. Like the Hunting Gate companies in England, both Californian companies concern themselves with factories, offices – especially offices – and shops but not, as yet, with housing, because it is extremely expensive and competition would be intense. The business is still small, with nothing like the elaborate organisation that has been built up in England, but California is one of the world's great growth areas, particularly in high technology, and Hunting Gate Pacific, with young management and an office in the heart of San Francisco's financial district, seems well placed to grow with it.

Our scene is set.

We have a picture of a business in property development which has risen from foundations laid about 35 years ago by an ex-subject of the Austrian Emperor, a lawyer by profession, who arrived in England in 1939. He is still the major shareholder, but the business is run nowadays by managers whom he took into his employment before it took its present form and whom he has since admitted to a share in the ownership. He founded the business in Hitchin – not the most likely of all places to choose, especially for an émigré from Central Europe – and its activities have spread about Great Britain and, under the founder's influence, to California as well. In recent years the business has been growing very fast indeed, but by methods necessarily different from those which the founder originally followed.

Hunting Gate Group, like most businesses, is a personal creation. Let us turn to consider the person who created it.

Chapter Two

FROM THE AUSTRIAN EMPIRE TO THE THIRD REICH 1916 - 1939

From the Austrian Empire to the Third Reich 1913 - 1939

IN 1913, when Frederick Bandet was born, the Dual Monarchy of Austria-Hungary bestrode Central Europe, having been put together over centuries as much by diplomatic marriages as by conquest. 'Alii bella gerunt', it used to be said, 'tu, felix Austria, nube'.* The Emperor of Austria was King of Hungary. In his Empire Germans and Magyars were dominant, but he ruled also over Italians, Serbs, Croats, Poles, Ruthenians, Rumanians, Czechs, Slovaks and Slovenes – all of them restless and resentful. Towards each other their ill-feeling was as great as it was towards their rulers but, as rulers, the Austrians stood out as targets for nationalists of every variety, and the Imperial Family was never safe, as Prinzep's shots at Serajevo, which precipitated the Great War, were soon to show.

The Dual Monarchy was new. It had been created, mainly for the benefit of the Germans and the Magyars, in 1867 but it had ancient roots. Austria – Oesterreich, the 'Eastern Realm' – stood for centuries as Europe's defender against the Turks, and as late as 1683 Sultan Mohamed IV besieged Vienna. Moreover, as long as most of Germany was split into minor states, Austria was unquestionably the leading German Power, despite the insolence of Prussia. Then, in the 19th century, with Turkey far gone in decline, Austria's great historic role seemed to have lost its meaning. With contemptuous ease, in the Seven Weeks' War of 1866, the Prussians displaced Austria at the head of Germany and went on, in 1871, to appropriate the adjective 'German' for their own newly founded Empire. Meanwhile, throughout the century, nationalist stirrings against Austrian rule gave Austria a bad name among liberals in Europe and America, and began sapping the

*Let others wage wars – you, blessed Austria, marry!

Europe in 1914.

foundations of the State. Austria-Hungary, in its latter days, has been described as 'despotism tempered with inefficiency'. Its despotism, by later standards, was mild, and its inefficiency was mingled with charm. Vienna, with its social life, its cafés, above all its music, was legendary.

Austria-Hungary was a great Power, ranking in Europe with the Russian Empire, the German Empire and the French Republic; in the world, with the British Empire and with the United States. The Dual Monarchy could put nearly two million men in the field in time of war. Its industrial power was far from negligible. Moreover the sad old Emperor Franz Josef II, who had come to the throne in 1848, could still inspire strong loyalty in his German subjects. 'This would never have happened', Frederick Bandet's maternal grandfather would say, if he disapproved of something, 'in the old Emperor's day.' By race and, temperately, by religion, the Bandets were Jewish but, in Frederick's early childhood, the branch of the family to which he belonged was German in language and culture and, in national loyalty, unreservedly Austrian.

The first Bandet of whom there is any record prospered first as a bookbinder, later as a dealer in ladies' dress materials, in the city of Cracow, which after 1846 belonged to the Austrian Empire. This business was eventually taken over by the founder's eldest son, Johan (born 1852), who is said to have been 'hard-working, methodical and extremely cautious.' Caution did not prevent him from expanding the retail business and buying, first, the house in which it had always been carried on, and then neighbouring properties. Any space he did not need for retailing, he divided, combined and re-combined into flats which eventually came to yield a considerable income. No doubt on the principle of spreading his risks, he used to keep

Emperor Franz Josef II 1830-1916 Reigned 1848-1916

one-third of his capital in the retail business, one-third in gold, and one-third in property. Caution and property, it seems, run in Frederick Bandet's blood.

Johan Bandet married Mina Haniser. They had three children: Heinrich (Henry) (1878 - 1944), Francisca (1883 - 1942), and Maximilian (1885 - 1957). Soon after Maximilian was born, his mother developed tuberculosis. It was incurable. She spent years in a sanatorium in the mountains of Styria, about sixty miles west of Vienna. In 1889 she died there leaving Johan with three young children. He soon re-married: a disaster for the children because the new wife seems to have been a stepmother in the worst sense.

Henry Bandet, eleven years old when his mother died, greatly wished to become a doctor or a lawyer. His younger brother Maximilian studied in Vienna, became a civil engineer, and rose high in the Austrian State Railway Service, in charge of the design of bridges, tunnels and permanent way in difficult subsoil conditions. For the elder son, Johan Bandet would allow no such career. He was conscripted, at the age of sixteen, into the family business, and there he stayed until 1912. Then, at the age of thirty-four, he married Regina Landerer (1887-1944), an extremely competent amateur painter who also had a good singing voice. Her parents were in business in Troppau in Silesia. In 1913, Henry and Regina became the parents of Frederick Bandet.

In many marriages, one partner is absorbed into the family of the other, and so it seems to have been for Henry Bandet. For him, perhaps, marriage provided an escape route from his stepmother, and from a business which he had never wanted to go into. As soon as he married, he moved to Troppau, and there he joined his father-in-law's firm.

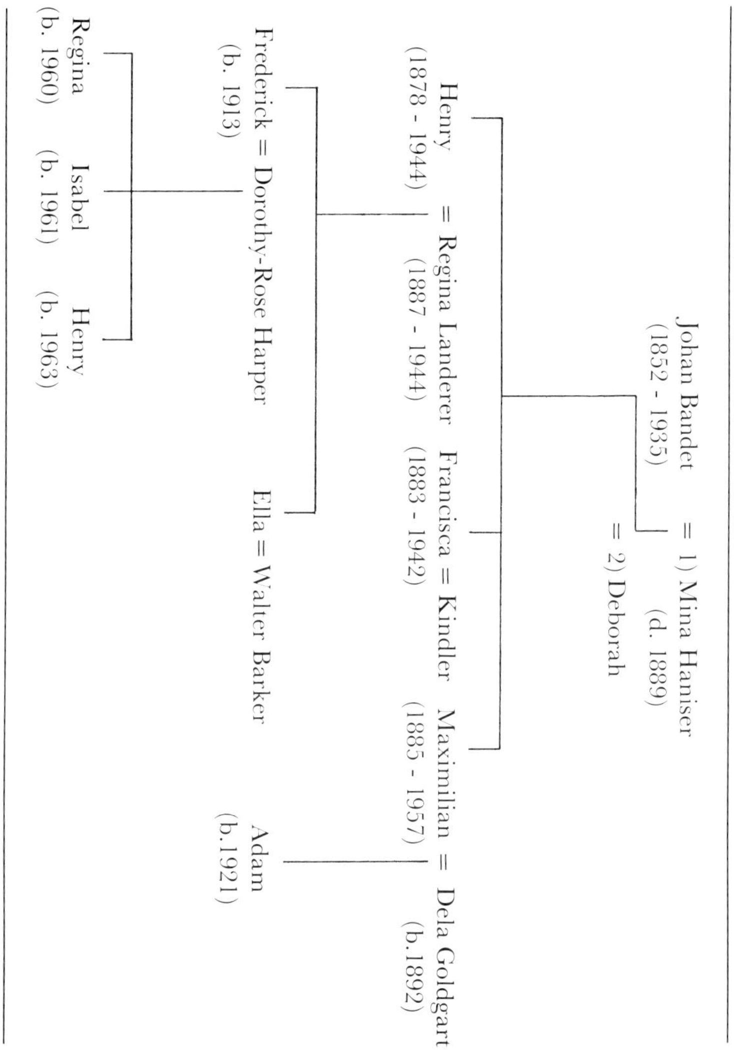
Johan Bandet (1852 - 1935) = 1) Mina Haniser (d. 1889)
= 2) Deborah
Henry (1878 - 1944) = Regina Landerer (1887 - 1944)
Francisca (1883 - 1942) = Kindler
Maximilian (1885 - 1957) = Dela Goldgart (b.1892)
Frederick (b. 1913) = Dorothy-Rose Harper
Ella = Walter Barker
Adam (b.1921)
Regina (b. 1960)
Isabel (b. 1961)
Henry (b. 1963)

Johan Bandet, Frederick Bandet's paternal grandfather, aged about 48.

Henry Bandet 1878-1944

Regina Bandet 1887-1944

Moses Landerer (1864-1929), and his wife Josefine (1867-1936) were to loom large in the childhood of their grandson, Frederick. They were the 'undoubted Heads', he says, 'of a large and close-knit family comprising two generations . . . I remember my grandfather, as did many others, as a particularly cheerful, happy and contented man. My bright blue eyes and pinkish complexion came from him and have been inherited by my elder daughter, Gina. He never ceased to joke of the good old days under the Emperor. He had none of the ceaseless drive and ambition that typifies men in business, and men who achieve success in most other fields. He was proud of his family and particularly proud of Alois, his successful eldest son; he was proud of Austria; he was proud of Germany. At times he and his wife, my grandmother, were invited by Alois to Breslau in Germany, and his pride in all that he perceived was such that it was rumoured that he had uttered the wish to be buried in German soil.'

Alois owned sawmills in Germany, supported by a programme of tree-farming which replaced felled trees with saplings to renew the forest. Ex-Kaiser Wilhelm II, living in exile in Holland after the Great War, employed Alois to manage the Hohenzollern forests in Germany. Small Frederick would occasionally see Uncle Alois arrive at Troppau in a vastly impressive equipage – a Packard limousine upholstered in royal blue velvet, with roller blinds to the windows, tip-up seats and speaking tubes from the back seats to Herr Pfeifer, the uniformed chauffeur.

Moses Landerer's business, which he had founded, supplied shoemakers with leather and everything else, except machinery, which they needed in their trade. The firm's representatives called on customers throughout the country. Competition from machine-made shoes, it seems, was not severe in pre-1914 Austria

A painting by Regina Bandet, copied from the work of an unidentified artist, with cups and saucers painted and signed by her.

Frederick Bandet's parents photographed in 1912, when Henry Bandet was 34 and his wife Regina was 25.

– not, at any rate, at the top end of the market which Landerer supplied. In the twenties, a Czech shoemaker called Thomas Bata brought American methods to his factory at Zlin, driving hand craftsmen out of business in their hundreds, but that was still in the future, long after Henry Bandet joined his father-in-law's firm.

The ownership and management of the business, naturally, were firmly in the hands of the Landerers and their connections by marriage. Moses took his youngest son, Simon, into partnership when he set the business up, and then, as his three daughters married, each son-in-law was successively admitted. They were Leopold Hilfstein, Marcus Mannheimer and Henry Bandet. Each brought capital with him.

Frederick Bandet, then, was born into a close-knit and apparently harmonious alliance between four families – Landerers, Hilfsteins, Mannheimers, Bandets – of the Austrian *bourgeoisie*. They were connected by marriage, united in business. They were comfortably off. Their place in the middle ranks of the ordered society of pre-1914 Austria must have seemed rock-solid. Any uneasiness they may have had about anti-semitism, which was never very far below the surface in Austria and Germany, does not seem to have been acute. Political disturbances – revolution – no doubt they dreaded, but there had been such disturbances in the past and they had survived. There might even be war. It was very close in 1908, and in 1913 the Balkans were aflame, but many well-informed people held the view that there could never be war between Great Powers again, or that if there was, it could not last long. Modern weapons and tactics would see to that and, besides, no Power, not even the wealthiest, not even Great Britain perhaps, would be able to afford a long war. Baby Frederick's future must have looked

Moses and Josefine Landerer, Frederick Bandet's maternal grandparents. Also shown in this photograph is Lilly, daughter of Alois.

Marcus Mannheimer, the partner of Henry Bandet.

very secure.....

In 1913, Troppau, his birthplace, was in Austrian Silesia, once part of the Duchy of Silesia. The whole Duchy was Austrian until, in 1740, Frederick the Great invaded it and annexed most of it to Prussia, thereby provoking two great European wars in the mid-years of the 18th century. The country round Troppau is mountainous and readily defensible, which was, doubtless, why the Austrians succeeded in holding Lower Silesia, with Troppau as its capital, when Upper Silesia was lost. In the late 1930's Lower Silesia acquired a melancholy fame as part of the Sudetenland, and played a large part in provoking the Second World War.

In 1913 the Austrians and the Prussians, though scarcely friends, were allies and the Czechs were Austrian subjects. The German Troppauers – that is, the majority of the town's inhabitants – had no cause to look nervously across the border and were masters in their own city, which was the provincial capital. As such, it had a large official and military element in its population of about 30,000 people. Woollen and linen fabrics were made there, so were sugar and liqueurs. Civil servants found it an agreeable place for retirement.

One day in October 1918, Frederick Bandet, five years old, came home as usual for lunch from his kindergarten. When he went back, the big front door was closed and he couldn't get in. Nor could one or two other children. They asked a passer-by why the door was shut. 'Don't you know?' was the reply. 'The Czechs have moved in.'

And so they had. Three Czech armies, fighting for the Allies, had persuaded Great Britain, the United States and other Powers to throw their weight behind the Czech demand for

Europe 1919 – 1938

independence. On 14th October 1918 the Czechoslovak National Council, in Prague, became the provisional government of Czechoslovakia and one of the ripples from that event, no doubt, closed small Frederick's kindergarten. The end of centuries of Hapsburg rule was orderly and bloodless. Austrian garrisons peaceably withdrew and, on 16th November 1918, the National Assembly in Prague decided on a republican form of government for Czechoslovakia and elected a Cabinet under Garrigue Masaryk. The new state was launched.

Thus the Bandets and their relations ceased to be subjects of an Empire with roots running back into the distant past, and became instead citizens of a brand new republic, created according to unimpeachable principles of self-determination. The Bandets did not particularly like their new nationality and remained, in sentiment, thoroughly Austrian, but they could not complain of oppression, for the government of the new state was a showpiece of liberal democracy. Czech officials in Troppau behaved with restraint. The singing of the old Austrian anthem, to Haydn's tune which was also used for *Deutschland über Alles*, was forbidden but the Germans kept their schools and their national customs, including occasional parades through the town. The Czech garrison looked the other way and, similarly, the Germans ignored the Czech garrison.

Frederick Bandet and his younger sister, Ellie, remember Troppau, provincial but cultured, as a pleasant town to grow up in. There were parks, gardens, swimming pools, tennis courts. The mountains were not far away and in winter there would be skiing. A theatre served also as an opera house and there was a concert hall.

On Sunday afternoons in the nineteen-twenties various members of the four inter-related families – Landerers, Bandets,

Frederick Bandet with his parents, 1914.

Schulring 13, Troppau. On 3rd Oct 1913, Frederick Bandet was born in an apartment on the 1st floor of this block over looking a park which follows the line of the old town defences.

Hilfsteins, Mannheimers – would gather at Hansl's coffee house. Henry Bandet would go ahead to read the papers which Hansl's provided – a service long since given up by similar establishments in England. Frederick particularly remembers his cousin, John Manford (Mannheimer), at these gatherings and they still reminisce together when they meet in London about the gorgeous Central European confections, smothered in cream, to which the children were treated. The children would be despatched to be entertained and at the same time to learn geography by gazing through stereoscopic binoculars – up to twenty-five viewers could be accommodated at a time – at hand-coloured photographs presenting panoramic views of some foreign country. 'Then', says Frederick Bandet, 'we rejoined the rest of the family in the coffee house completely oblivious of the smoke-filled atmosphere.' Since then he has developed an almost obsessive intolerance of smoking which he does not hesitate to express wherever he happens to be.

Frederick Bandet had the education normal, in his day, for a boy of good natural abilities in Central Europe. From 1923 to 1931 he attended the German State Gymnasium – the nearest English equivalent would be a grammar school – in Troppau. In three hundred years of existence – it was founded in the 17th century – its most distinguished pupil had been J.G.Mendel (1822-1884), the Augustinian Abbot of peasant origins who laid the foundations of the science of genetics by studying the reproductive cycle of plants.

The curriculum at the Gymnasium was solidly and severely classical. From the age of ten to the age of eighteen, Frederick Bandet had an hour of Latin and an hour of Greek almost every day, and he still has better Latin than most people. French and English were learnt privately. The school prepared its pupils

The Schlesische Landesmuseum, a museum in Troppau.

The Theatre/Opera House in Troppau.

Frederick Bandet and his sister Ellie in 1920.

for the *'Matura'*, a leaving examination roughly equivalent to the GCE at 'A' Level or the French *Baccalauréat,* so that they could go on to the university to read medicine, law, philosophy or theology. No other possibilities were entertained.

From the master who taught German Literature came a sinister hint of things to come. He was a fanatical German nationalist and anti-semitic as well, though he always behaved correctly towards Frederick Bandet. In his teaching he propagated the idea of Greater Germany – including Austria and the Sudetenland – and anti-Jewish prejudice too. In the middle of one of his lessons he said something about 'the Einstein theory, which in its day created so much dust', implying that the theory was discredited. He left no doubt in one young mind, however, that his real objection to Einstein's theory was not scientific but racial. In this way, several years before Hitler came to power in Germany, Nazi doctrine was being preached in a school in Czechoslovakia.

Frederick and his cousins, sons of the other partners in the family business, were introduced very early to a business atmosphere. The sisters who were their mothers would bring the boys to the firm's offices at the end of the working day – about six to half-past six in the evening – and then sit chatting while they waited for their husbands. Frederick, tolerated by his father in his office, would watch Henry walking up and down the room, dictating to his secretary, Miss Kaufmann. He must have been among the earliest business men to have a woman as a secretary, for the job was almost always held by a man before 1914 and very commonly later. The letters often dealt with disputes between the firm and its customers which would eventually become the subject of personal negotiations. It gradually became apparent to the listening boy that, as he says, 'it was worthwhile to bargain over a *heller,* namely the hundredth

Frederick Bandet's school, the German State Gymnasium in Troppau. This building was put up in 1869-70 and badly damaged in 1945.

part of a crown, or *krone*, when thousands of square feet of leather were concerned.' He taught himself to type on Miss Kaufmann's spare machine, but only with two fingers.

Between 1923 and 1928, Simon Landerer and Leopold Hilfstein died, and Moses Landerer died in 1929, leaving Marcus Mannheimer and Henry Bandet in charge of Hilfstein & Landerer's business. By this time Bata was flooding the market with cheap, ready-made shoes which must have been very damaging to the trade in leather for expensive, hand-made shoes. For this reason, probably, Mannheimer and Bandet decided to move out of trading in leather and into the manufacture of leather goods.

This looks like a bold decision, forced on them by circumstances. Leather they knew, but of production processes for such things as briefcases, wallets and note cases they had no experience. They needed a technical partner, and they found one in Anton Malek. He owned a leather goods shop where he traded under his own name, making many of his goods himself in a small workshop at the rear of his premises, and buying some in.

Hilfstein & Landerer closed down in about 1932 or 1933. Henry Bandet, Marcus Mannheimer and Anton Malek formed a partnership, each partner having a one-third interest. Bandet and Mannheimer brought capital; Malek, skill and technical knowledge. His specialities, apart from briefcases, were wallets and note cases which were more and more in demand alongside leather handbags which had become popular much earlier. The firm was called A. Malek & Co. It soon prospered sufficiently for the partners to take over a former textile factory, the Silesia Works, near Troppau railway station. The new blood which came into the partnership brought new ideas, encouraged expansion. Together, the three men identified openings in the market which other and larger firms had not filled. The capital brought in by Bandet and Mannheimer enabled the firm to start exporting to various European countries throughout the thirties, giving evidence of the vigorous spirit of enterprise widespread in Czechoslovakia during its brief existence – a mere twenty years – as an independent state.

Neither Frederick nor his cousins saw anything of production because they were barred from the factory during working hours. Nevertheless Frederick came to know the firm's products

General view of Vienna showing the spire of St. Stephen's, 1920.

very well, and when he went to other towns he would look for them in the best shops. 'It made my day', he says, 'when I recognised our products in a window. Prague, Vienna and other towns became happy hunting grounds for the opportunity for quiet self-admiration.'

The Bandet family moved in circles in which parents commonly hoped to see their sons become either doctors or lawyers. No one seems to have pressed Frederick to go into the family business. This seems strange, since he was the only son, but it would not have been his own wish and perhaps his father remembered his own experience too vividly to thrust Frederick into a career which he had no desire to enter.

The young man's inclination lay towards the law, and in 1931 he went to the ancient Charles University of Prague.

Frederick Bandet in 1931 when he entered Charles University, Prague.

Wenzels Platz, the main square in Prague.

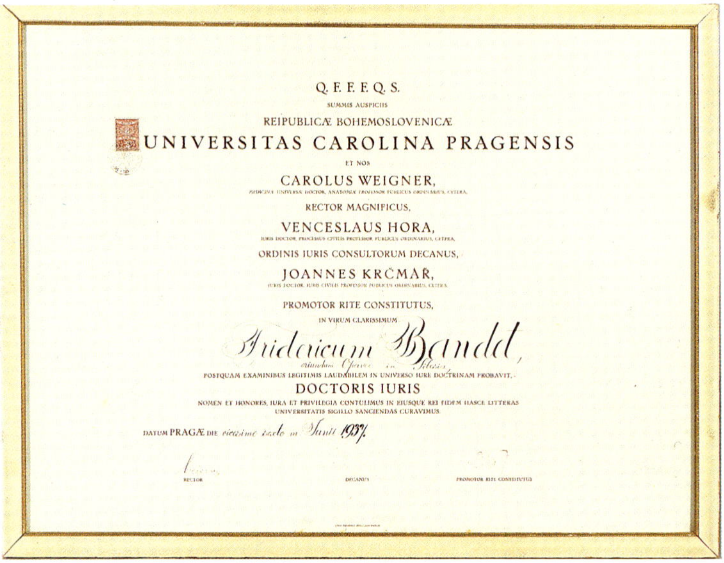

Q. F. F. F. Q. S.
SUMMIS AUSPICIIS
REIPUBLICÆ BOHEMOSLOVENICÆ
UNIVERSITAS CAROLINA PRAGENSIS
ET NOS
CAROLUS WEIGNER,
MEDICINÆ UNIVERSÆ DOCTOR, ANATOMIÆ PROFESSOR PUBLICUS ORDINARIUS, CETERA,
RECTOR MAGNIFICUS,
VENCESLAUS HORA,
IURIS DOCTOR, PROCESSUS CIVILIS PROFESSOR PUBLICUS ORDINARIUS, CETERA,
ORDINIS IURIS CONSULTORUM DECANUS,
JOANNES KRČMAŘ,
IURIS DOCTOR, IURIS CIVILIS PROFESSOR PUBLICUS ORDINARIUS, CETERA,
PROMOTOR RITE CONSTITUTUS,
IN VIRUM CLARISSIMUM
Fridericum Bandet,
oriundum Opavae in Silesia,
POSTQUAM EXAMINIBUS LEGITIMIS LAUDABILEM IN UNIVERSO IURE DOCTRINAM PROBAVIT,
DOCTORIS IURIS
NOMEN ET HONORES, IURA ET PRIVILEGIA CONTULIMUS IN EIUSQUE REI FIDEM HASCE LITTERAS
UNIVERSITATIS SIGILLO SANCIENDAS CURAVIMUS.
DATUM PRAGÆ DIE *vicesimo sexto m Junii 1937.*

RECTOR DECANUS PROMOTOR RITE CONSTITUTUS

The certificate for the degree of LLD which Frederick Bandet gained from Charles University in 1937. It now hangs in his office in Menlo Park, California.

Instead of studying in his mother tongue, German, he worked and took his exams in Czech, which meant continual reference to a dictionary, a most laborious process. Nevertheless, he found time to enjoy himself. The climax of the social season was a ball in the tradition of the Vienna Opera Ball, and he spent several months organising that. At weekends he would go into the country, skiing during the winter in the Sudeten mountains north of Prague. For variety he sometimes went to lectures in the medical faculty, and he took two semesters of forensic medicine – morbid, but fascinating. His interests were intellectual and musical; he read widely and went to the opera.

In 1937 he passed his third oral exam, the *Rigorosum*, with high honours and he knew his degree – LLD – was safe. He sent his parents and sister a long telegram of thanks for their support. 'Wie vier', he said, 'sind eins'.

Now he had his reward. If his qualification had been gained in German he would have found employment difficult to get. As it was, a law firm in Prague (Dr. Raudnitzky & Co.) took him on, which was no doubt a good bargain for both sides. Frederick got a job and the firm, a conscientious young man. His Czech was imperfect, but he stayed with the firm until early in 1939, when his legal career was overwhelmed by events. Since then, Frederick Bandet has always been his own employer.

By the beginning of 1938 the last days of liberal Czechoslovakia were very close. Hitler, ruler of Germany since January 1933, was giving ample evidence of his aggressive intentions and of his malevolence towards the Jews. More and more were leaving Germany, if they could, in yet another mass exodus, the latest in a long succession since Moses had led Israel out of Egypt three thousand years before.

The Germans in Silesia had never liked Czech rule. That was understandable, since it had been thrust upon them without their consent sought or given. During the late thirties their leader, Konrad Henlein, began to press their grievances – which were not all imaginary – and by 1938 he had Hitler's overt backing. The Czechs could not contemplate surrendering Silesia to Germany, since that would ruin their frontier defences and, as late as May, Henlein was not openly demanding outright union with Germany; merely, as he told Churchill, 'local autonomy', with

Czech troops in the fortresses and Prague in control of defence, finance, foreign policy and communications. As the summer went on, however, it became clear that no concessions the Czechs felt able to make – and they made a great many – would content Henlein or his master. Czechoslovakia must fall.

To one young man in Silesia, Frederick Bandet, the situation looked threatening enough for him to consider a family move to England. No doubt he was mindful not only of Hitler's increasing raucousness and Henlein's growing arrogance, but also of the anti-semitism always discernible in Troppau.

The opportunity for moving to England was offered by a man called Whitehead, who was trying to attract foreign investment in the Team Valley Trading Estate near Newcastle-on-Tyne, set up under the National Government's programme for dealing with 'Special Areas'. There were also possibilities on another Trading Estate at Treforest in South Wales, not far from Cardiff.

To Frederick Bandet's elders, this idea was not welcome; indeed, it was inconceivable. Brought up, as they had been, in apparently unshakeable security, even the crash of the Austrian Empire, it seems, had not entirely disillusioned them, perhaps because their experience in Czechoslovakia had been so unalarming. They could see that the Germans seemed bemused by an evil lunatic, but they remained serenely confident that the Great Powers would know how to deal with him. Frederick, and those who thought like him, were hysterical scaremongers.

This mood, perhaps induced by a more or less conscious refusal to recognise the hideous face of truth, outlasted the creation of Greater Germany, brought about by the invasion of Austria – the *Anschluss* – in March 1938, after which Hitler could turn

The German invasion of Czechoslovakia. German troops entering Brno, Moravia on 17th March 1939.

his full attention to Czechoslovakia. A somewhat similar mood prevailed much longer in England. Recent memories of the Great War, barely twenty years in the past, combined with the dread of the still nameless horrors of aerial bombardment, perhaps with poison gas, to produce a kind of mental numbness, a refusal to face reality, in which fear was a large element, and which was not entirely dispelled until the heavens began to fall in the Spring of 1940.

The moment of ultimate truth came earlier in Czechoslovakia. At the end of September 1938, under pressure at Munich from the Great Powers, confronted with the growing threat of internal disruption, friendless in Central Europe, the Czech Government agreed to let the Germans into the Sudetenland. That destroyed the Czech defences, and the defenceless Czech state was itself destroyed a few months later. On 14th March 1939, German troops marched into Prague. The Slovaks declared their independence. Hungarians seized territory in the East. Hitler declared a Protectorate – ironic term – and the scene was set for the unhindered deployment of Nazi abominations.

After the Munich Agreement was signed in September 1938, but before the Germans moved into Silesia, the Bandets fled from Troppau, where they had spent their 26 years of married life. Sensible at last of danger, they went to a small town in Moravia called Prossnitz which was nearer to Prague, and Frederick's parents began seriously to consider leaving the country. All they needed was an exit visa, but this depended on satisfying the authorities that they had an entry visa to another country.

Frederick came to England in February 1939, to start negotiations for a factory, so that he was already there when the Germans entered Prague. After that his parents' difficulties became acute, for German exchange control prevented them taking funds out of Czecho-Slovakia (as the country's name was now spelt). Until they could bring funds with them the British authorities would not grant them an entry visa, and until they had an entry visa they were not allowed to leave Czecho-Slovakia. Breaking this malign circle and getting a British entry visa for his parents and sister began to override all other considerations in Frederick's mind. Time, perhaps, there still might be, but not very much.

Chapter Three

SURVIVAL
1939 – 1945

Survival 1939 – 1945

Frederick Bandet's situation in the Spring of 1939 was the most anguished it is possible to imagine. The German invasion of Czecho-Slovakia had thrown his parents and his sister into imminent danger. He was far from them, alone in a foreign country he had never visited before, a country in which the Prime Minister, after forcing the Czech Government into the Munich agreement, had referred to 'a quarrel in a faraway country between people of whom we know nothing'. A great, growing anxiety overhung him: would his parents and his sister get out of Czecho-Slovakia in time? Beside that question, the business which had brought him to England – negotiating for a factory – was of small account.

At the heart of the matter lay money. Frederick brought very little with him to England. Such funds as the family were ultimately able to transfer had to be got out of occupied Czecho-Slovakia illegally and in small sums into Switzerland and thence to England. It was only when the family could satisfy the Home Office that they had sufficient means that the officials would consider granting the visas which the Bandet family so desperately needed. All this took time. At length, in June, money arrived in London. The Home Office issued visas in August.

That was too late. War broke out and stopped Frederick Bandet's parents' coming. He tried to get them visas for Bolivia but that too failed. His sister survived the horrors which followed. His parents were killed in the gas chambers of Auschwitz. He has ever since been tormented by a nightmare: was it something he did or left undone, in the Spring of 1939, that caused the deadly delay? He developed an intense and permanent bitterness towards the nation which his grandfather had admired above all others, and if, today, he is introduced to a German he is inclined to remark 'I come from the Sudetenland; you may have heard of it'.

During these miserable months, Frederick Bandet lived in a boarding-house in South Kensington on next to nothing. Every penny, every pound he spent was that much less capital. He thinks he probably lived on less than £6 a week, including the rent of his room, and he soon stopped having breakfast. He did his own shopping and lived chiefly on cold food. He had no regular job, indeed no job at all, and practically no social life either. 'This', he says, 'was the other traumatic feature'. He formed one or two friendships with women but no more.

Military service might have been a relief, but he was unfit for it, having suffered for many years from curvature of the spine. It was so slight as to be barely noticeable, but it had been detected when he was eleven or twelve years old by a tailor making his first suit, and neither cause nor cure, in spite of every effort, was ever discovered. His parents were both healthy. They suffered no congenital disorders such as asthma, migraine or allergies. They were non-smokers, almost teetotallers. They treated their children's occasional ailments with concern and affection but they were confident of their general health. They were accordingly distressed almost to the point of desperation by Frederick's worsening problem. He became acutely conscious of it, and remains so, although the physical handicap, like the almost imperceptible disfigurement, is small. His business acquaintances sometimes find it disconcerting when he asks to lie down for an hour or so during the day but this is necessary in order to stretch his spine. It was not until the 1950's that a surgical operation was perfected which cures the complaint in adolescents safely and permanently.

Denied the possibility of military service, Frederick Bandet inhabited a suburban limbo of furnished rooms, evidently so greatly depressed that he no longer cared to think creatively. He moved from South Kensington to Golders Green, because it was cheaper. He stayed in Golders Green during the heavy bombing of 1940 - 41, because he didn't know what else to do. At length he decided that he might as well move away from London, but he had no clear idea where to go. He noticed Green Line buses going north. He got on one going to Baldock. He took a furnished room there, still relying on his diminishing capital. His misery was increased by the suspicion in which he was held as a German-speaking foreigner in a district where more than one case of espionage was uncovered.

Baldock is a market town in Hertfordshire, about 40 miles from London on the Great North Road, which at one time kept its inn-keepers busy. In 1940 it had about three to four thousand inhabitants and no particular claim to distinction. It was certainly not the most obvious place for an immigrant from Central Europe to choose to make a living in. Nevertheless, as soon as Frederick Bandet went to Baldock, the creative powers of his mind and the normally powerful thrust of his will began to assert themselves again. The pendulum of his fortunes, having swung very low, started to move upwards again.

Besides money, Bandet's father had sent machinery to England from the factory in Troppau, and when Frederick Bandet went to Baldock it was still in store, costing money but earning none. Could he put it to use? He knew nothing of the technology of his father's firm, but he could learn. He went to Foyles and picked up what he calls 'a fairly good book'. He joined an evening class run by the London County Council (the predecessor of the GLC) where they taught the manufacture of leather goods. It was in Southampton Row, London, opposite the colonnaded entrance to Sicilian Avenue. For nine months he went there twice a week – Mondays and Thursdays from 6 to 9 p.m. – through the blackout and the Blitz, travelling in from Baldock by train. Frederick Bandet's instinct for survival – and more than survival – was beginning to assert itself strongly.

He set about starting a small leather goods business. Some raw material he already had, because he had brought leather over from Czecho-Slovakia and in the early months of the war he had invested a substantial part of his family's capital in sealskin, crocodile skin and Morocco leather (goatskin), reasoning – correctly – that these purchases would protect his capital from the wartime inflation which he foresaw, and that fancy leathers such as these would not be considered so essential to the war effort as hides and would not, therefore, be requisitioned. From his reading and the evening classes he had gained the necessary knowledge for his proposed manufacturing activity. He still needed a Home Office work permit, people to work for him, and premises for them to work in.

The Home Office granted him the work permit he needed. He found women in Baldock with nothing to do, who were glad of a chance to earn money. He taught them the skill which he had so recently acquired, enabling them to make purses and wallets in their own homes, while he ran the business from his furnished room. Then he looked about for workshop premises. In Pond Lane, a side street near the George & Dragon Inn, he found a range of four garages, converted from stables, with a hayloft above which had remained unchanged with access via the traditional ladder only. He took the property on a short lease and found a builder to adapt it to his own purposes. Such

Frederick Bandet's first premises at Pond Lane, Baldock.

capital as was needed – it was not much – he found from his own resources: he did not borrow.

The builder, John Ray, was considerably older than Frederick Bandet, who found him 'an extremely charming and forthcoming talkative man.' He put plasterboard walls and a ceiling into the hayloft, producing a workshop at one end and a tiny flat at the other, with a bedroom, a living room and a bathroom. Bandet moved his machinery and a few employees – no more than three or four at first – into the workshop, himself into the flat, and launched the Banton Manufacturing Co Limited. He didn't use his own name. The word 'Bandet,' with a minimal change of spelling, gives rise to innumerable witticisms of greater or less brilliance in many languages. His father and grandfather had both suffered from them: he had no mind to – at least not for business purposes!

He went into business in 1941. Within a year or so the firm was self-supporting though probably – the accounts are lost – not much more. Towards the end of the war, in 1945, it was prosperous enough to provide employment for a few more women. Its range of products was modelled on the range produced at Troppau, but more limited.

While he was building his business, Frederick Bandet was also finding a place in the local community, largely through voluntary war work. Feeling a duty to serve, he offered to join the ambulance service, but he wasn't accepted because he couldn't drive. For some reason which he will never understand, he found himself in the Heavy Rescue Service, a branch of Civil Defence.

The service in Baldock was entirely staffed with local builders' men, and a more unsuitable service for anyone of Frederick Bandet's slender build and slight but definite physical handicap would have been hard to find. The men he worked with were all older than he was, but they were all used to climbing ladders, an experience which he found horrifying. They went for training to the local Fire Brigade's tower, and they were issued with a vast wardrobe of protective clothing, especially against gas. Only a few stray bombs fell on Baldock, and they were not often called out until right at the end of the war. Then flying bombs and V2 missiles began to come over, and although none came as far as Baldock, they took turns in manning the station at night, either to help in Baldock itself or on standby for London.

In 1945, as Germany and Japan successively collapsed and warfare ceased, the owners of the range of garages in Baldock where Banton Manufacturing was established began to press for possession of their property, in its improved state. Their legal position was strong and, on the face of it, Frederick Bandet was presented with a potentially disastrous situation, for he would not easily find a new home for his infant business. Certainly there would be no hope of putting up a new building, which was what he really wanted, without official permission – so tight, wide and detailed was the official grip on the war economy – and official permission would be hard to get. What the authorities would look at would not be a young man struggling to establish himself, but the demand he would be making on resources of labour and materials which were extremely scarce. Without skilful and persistent advocacy there was not much doubt that Frederick Bandet's case would fail.

Bandet had strong nerves, a strong will, and considerable skill, learnt from his employer in Prague, in putting a case to the authorities, whom he did not find very different in England from those he had been used to in Czecho-Slovakia. It was a matter of combining a dry, impersonal, professional approach with a suggestion that the applicant's situation was so heart-rending as to deserve special treatment. What could be more heart-rending than the threat to turn him out of the garage block in Baldock? He faced his encounter with the authorities with confidence, prepared to meet the most threatening aspect of his situation head on and turn it to his advantage.

He needed a site. His local associations, newly formed, were helpful, for with introductions from John Ray he began looking at plots of land. The most likely possibility seemed to be not in Baldock, but in Hitchin, about five or six miles to the South West. Hitchin is a good deal larger than Baldock. When Frederick Bandet first went there, it had 19,960 inhabitants. Thirty years later, it had 30,320. It is an ancient, agreeable market town, already old by the time the Domesday Book was compiled, which grew up in the distant past alongside a tiny river, the Hiz, and at the junction of several roads, none of more than local importance but sufficient collectively to channel trade into the town. Like many other English towns of the same kind, its long, placid history is distinguished by a total lack of distinction, and the earlier phases of the industrial revolution passed it by. It lies in gently rolling farmland below the Northern edge of the Chilterns, and today its pleasant situation and ready access to good communications, particularly with London, make it an attractive place in which to live, to work, or to set up a factory.

In a road called Wilbury Way to the North of the town, on land originally intended for housing, a factory making goods essential for the war effort had been put up after the firm's London premises had been bombed, thus opening up the area for industrial development. The land belonged to a local farmer,

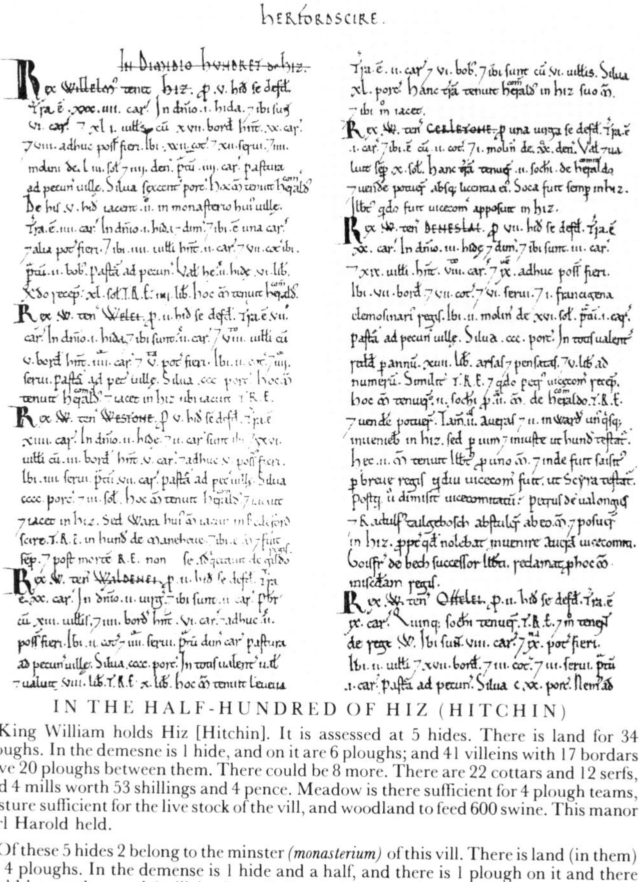

IN THE HALF-HUNDRED OF HIZ (HITCHIN)

King William holds Hiz [Hitchin]. It is assessed at 5 hides. There is land for 34 ploughs. In the demesne is 1 hide, and on it are 6 ploughs; and 41 villeins with 17 bordars have 20 ploughs between them. There could be 8 more. There are 22 cottars and 12 serfs, and 4 mills worth 53 shillings and 4 pence. Meadow is there sufficient for 4 plough teams, pasture sufficient for the live stock of the vill, and woodland to feed 600 swine. This manor earl Harold held.

Of these 5 hides 2 belong to the minster *(monasterium)* of this vill. There is land (in them) for 4 ploughs. In the demense is 1 hide and a half, and there is 1 plough on it and there could be another; and 4 villeins have 2 ploughs between them, and there are 7 cottars. Meadow is there sufficient for 2 oxen, pasture sufficient for the live stock. These 2 hides are worth 6 pounds; when received they were worth 40 shillings; *in the time of King Edward (1066) worth 4 pounds.* This manor Earl Harold held.

Entry in the Domesday Book referring to Hitchin circa 1085.
By courtesy of The British Library.

William Wallace, and the plot that Frederick Bandet sought to buy was priced at about £350 for 1/4 acre. William Wallace came to Frederick Bandet's office in Baldock to discuss the matter. Bandet pointed out that the shape of the plot was awkward. Wallace walked up and down the room, then stopped. 'You know, Frederick,' he said, looking at him, 'my father has now been dead these fifteen years, but if he knew' – his glance turned Heavenward – 'if he knew that I was giving something away for a penny less than I could get for it' – he again looked up – 'he would never forgive me'. This speech abruptly ended any haggling over the price. Bandet agreed to the figure Wallace asked.

Negotiations with the authorities, even more important than negotiations with the owner of the land, were not so easily concluded. Everything needed a permit or a licence, on top of planning permission and bye-law permission. There were monetary restrictions as well: only a specified sum might be spent each year, and unspent balances could not be carried over.

The officials in charge of these matters were in Cambridge, some 25 miles North East of Baldock. Frederick Bandet, having learnt to drive, provided himself in 1946 with his first car, a small Standard, and combined his written approaches with assiduous personal attendance at the Government offices in the southern outskirts of Cambridge. In the corridors where he waited he remembers elderly men in messengers' uniforms pushing tea trolleys, very slowly, with expressions of heavenly content on their faces. Could this be a vision of Paradise?

Whether it was Paradise or not, practical realities had to be faced. The landlord of the Pond Lane property, all unknowing, was of great assistance. His continual pressure to regain possession of his property, including requests for signed declarations

Park Street, Hitchin in 1920.

This photograph shows how little the scene has changed over the past 60 years. In 1981 a new headquarters was completed for Hunting Gate Homes, Hitchin (just visible at the end of the row).

by Frederick Bandet (which Bandet never made) that he was intending to get out voluntarily by a certain date, was of great help in building up Bandet's case to the authorities in Cambridge.

There remained the problem of finding a builder. Through service with Heavy Rescue Frederick Bandet had got to know a local builder called Rabone who struck him as amiable and well educated. When the proposition of building a leather goods factory was put to Rabone he said: 'You know, Mr. Bandet, you could just as well build it yourself.'

This was a turning point in Frederick Bandet's career, though he didn't recognise it at the time. His impression was that Rabone, contemplating the morass of red tape he would have to wade through, decided that the job wasn't worth his while. As far as Bandet was concerned, at that time, Rabone might just as well have told him to fly over the moon. It did not occur to him, then, that he could build anything, and he was used to conditions widespread in Continental Europe under which no one could set up as a builder without appropriate professional qualifications.

Rabone's remark, nevertheless, widened Bandet's horizons. John Ray refused the job, too. At that time of chronic shortage and innumerable licences, neither he nor Rabone liked the idea of having to get all the materials together and perhaps the job was too small to interest them. Ray, in his late sixties, was by this time more of a property owner than a builder and he didn't want to get involved. He did, however, introduce Bandet to an architect.

This architect did a lot of local authority work. He may even have been employed by the local authority, with freedom to work independently as well. He prepared plans for Frederick

Bandet's project and he got planning permission but, before work could start, steel was needed for the frame of the building, which had to be pre-fabricated. The architect negotiated the job with a London firm, then sent Bandet an order for him to sign. On it the fabricators gave, as a delivery date, 'three months after receipt of licence and steel.'

Frederick Bandet was not much worried by the prospect of getting the licence: that he could control. The steel was a different matter. Again and again he telephoned the fabricators, but they were non-commital as to when they would get it and they didn't seem very interested. They said they couldn't promise any date. When Bandet informed his architect of his unwillingness to sign an order without a delivery date he was told that there was no alternative. Bandet then consulted Stent Pre-Cast Products, who made pre-cast concrete beams. They only needed steel for reinforcement and they were perfectly willing to quote a delivery date.

The architect, faced with this proposition, told Bandet over the phone that he didn't intend to lose face with his suppliers. Bandet said he was going ahead anyway. After that the architect wrote to say that he wouldn't have his name associated with an architectural abomination such as pre-cast concrete and in accordance with standard RIBA terms, a copy of which he enclosed, he claimed his fee. Bandet sent him his fee and thanked him for his services. 'Ever since', he says, 'I have remained a bad client, but a good employer of architects.' Architects, it is to be hoped, would agree.

Frederick Bandet now had plans but he still needed a builder, although he was feeling his way towards building himself. At the offices of Hitchin Urban District Council he met the surveyor, Anthony King. King advised against building a factory in Hitchin where he thought there would be difficulties in finding labour. Nevertheless, he recommended consulting Albert Haley, clerk of the works for the first council houses built in Hitchin after the war.

Haley, a blunt Yorkshireman, had bright blue eyes, red cheeks and fair hair. He had at one time been in the Royal Navy. He was entirely self-taught, and how he had become such a jack-of-all-trades, including music, as he was, Bandet never quite found out. Haley often talked of the happy times he had spent, with his family, working on oil installations in Persia.

Haley had a positive attitude to everything, very refreshing after the architect. Bandet felt that if he asked Haley to stand a pyramid on its head he would manage it, instead of proving that it couldn't be done. He had a full-time job with the Council, but the surveyor raised no objection to his spare time activities, even if they resembled his professional duties. He arranged the purchase of a concrete mixer. He knew plenty of men willing to start on the foundations and other works and he told Bandet what to order and what to do in the daytime. In the evening Bandet reported back to him, and so the work went on. He and Bandet regularly spent almost all their evenings together – Haley had one of the first Hitchin post-war council houses in Girdle Road, a side street off Wilbury Way – which made supervision easy during the light evenings of summer. Bandet himself was also by this time living in Hitchin in a newly built house rented to him by John Ray, and he had a flat in London as well.

Bandet's new factory had a single storey with a pitched roof providing extra height for storage, and there were two or three offices. It was a long time a-building. A stream of licences had to be obtained, necessitating frequent visits by Bandet to

The first factory built by Frederick Bandet in Wilbury Way, Hitchin.

Cambridge, and expenditure had to be very carefully watched because it was closely controlled, with narrow limits on how much might be spent in a year. Frederick Bandet financed the building: he did not borrow.

In 1949, to the relief of his landlords, Bandet moved his business out of Pond Lane, Baldock, and into the new factory in Hitchin. Then, as he had suspected all along, he found that the leather goods business wasn't really for him. Competition was

Skiing at Zermatt, 1950.

becoming stronger, and he had discovered in himself a passion for building, which later he expressed in a slogan on his letter-head: *Vita nova in aedificiis novis*. He was eventually persuaded to drop it because so few people understood what it meant.* That was a pity, because it expressed Frederick Bandet's feelings perfectly. Constructive thinking and construction, to his mind, go together.

He soon closed down leather goods production. Then he watched property prices in *The Times* and the *Daily Telegraph* and asked a leading firm of London agents what his factory would be likely to fetch. The price they suggested seemed to him low. He advertised in the *Evening Standard* and before long an ice-cream maker offered what he was asking: to the best of his recollection, £8,250.

It was a fabulous sum of money. As Bandet went to collect the cheque from his solicitors – Messrs. Heckford, Norton in Letchworth – he was in a seventh heaven of delight, feeling that he had so much enjoyed the job that he shouldn't really have been paid at all. It was all too good to be true and downstairs there was a branch of W.H. Smith with a book in the window called *All This and Heaven Too*. He bought the book and he still has it. What it was about he has forgotten, but at the moment the title expressed his feelings perfectly. He had found his vocation.

*'New life in new buildings'.

Chapter Four

THE MAKING OF A PROPERTY DEVELOPER

The making of a property developer

THE plan which began to form in Frederick Bandet's mind as his first factory rose from the ground alongside Wilbury Way was to build more factories, not for sale but for letting, keeping the ownership in his own hands. He would thus build up, in time, an array of the most solid assets it is possible to own: land and buildings. These assets, unlike some other forms of personal wealth, would generate income, and if the leases were drawn with due allowance for periodical review of the rents they would generate increasing income.

Nor was this all. Provided that Frederick Bandet chose factory sites judiciously in the first place, and provided that his property, as it accumulated, was properly managed, with proper attention to the choice of tenants and to the upkeep and obsolescence of the buildings, there was no reason why his property should not go on producing income as far into the future as anyone cared to look, as the estates of the landed gentry had done for generations past. Not only Bandet himself, but any family he might found, would be as well provided for as forethought could arrange.

There was nothing speculative about these plans, except insofar as all planning must be an exercise in balancing uncertainties and no business enterprise is without risk. There are, however, degrees and kinds of risk. Frederick Bandet did not set out to be a trader in property, seeking profit by shrewd purchase, rapid development, and immediate sale. He is by nature cautious and his whole policy has from the first been founded on caution: to build up a position and consolidate it before moving towards the next. Rather than trying to run fast, he has preferred to move slowly and have no setbacks, remaining always well within the range of resources available to him and avoiding any more risk than he has been confident of being able to control. 'You can accept the breaking of a piece of china', he says, 'if you do it yourself: it is very different if some one else breaks it, which is a risk beyond your own control. If someone else takes risks for you, that's when I get nervous.'

It cannot be fanciful to perceive in Frederick Bandet's approach to business a deep craving for security, deriving from such a state of insecurity as no native-born Englishman has been called upon to endure. An instinct of this kind is discernible among Bandet's Jewish forebears in Central Europe in the mid-nineteenth century: is it remarkable that such an instinct should display itself again after his own experience in the fourth decade of the twentieth century?

His early plans were based on a realistic appraisal of possibilities in Hitchin. The Wallace family owned land on each side of Wilbury Way which they were willing to let or sell for development. Hitchin Urban District Council, glancing enviously at industrial development in nearby Letchworth, which had roughly the same population but ten times as much rateable industrial space, would be delighted to see an industrial estate take shape in Hitchin, because it would bring in so much extra income from rates (the equivalent of US property tax). An industrial estate was precisely what Frederick Bandet intended to create. It would have good connections by rail and road, it would be within easy reach of London and, it was reasonable to hope, labour would be readily available, though this opinion was not universally held.

In the years immediately after the war, however, there were formidable obstacles in the path of an intending property developer. The economy was still in the grip of a system of control which ramified into every nook and cranny of the national life, specifying not only how little 'carcass meat' and how few 'shell eggs' the citizen was allowed each week (the Ministry of Food had a vocabulary peculiarly its own, apparently designed to reduce appetite), but also prescribing the depth of water (five inches) the King should have in his bath. The system, set up by a Government in which the Conservative party was dominant, produced the perfect model of a centrally directed economy, paying not the slightest regard to market forces, and for its purpose–the organisation of victory–it was appropriate and efficient.

It was appropriate also, though progressively less so, in the years after the war when Frederick Bandet was launching his property enterprise. The incoming Labour Government, which was not ill-disposed to the notion of a centrally directed economy, was faced by a situation in which economic policy was dominated by the needs of the export trade, by a scarcity of dollars exacerbated by the sudden end of Lend-Lease in the summer of 1945, and by a determination to preserve the standing of sterling as an international reserve currency. The consequence in post-war England was that food and almost every other desirable commodity was 'in short supply' – a phrase as characteristic of the times as 'spiv' and 'black market'–and therefore rigidly controlled by some form of rationing or licensing.

Building was controlled partly by very tight limits on the sums of money that might be spent, from year to year, on any project, and partly by a licensing system for materials, especially steel, timber, bricks, glass and plasterboard. Moreover, whereas under the rationing regulations for food and clothing everyone had a right to certain minimum allowances, there was no such right under the building regulations. Every new project had to be justified to the Ministry of Works, which was the appropriate authority within the central Government, before officials

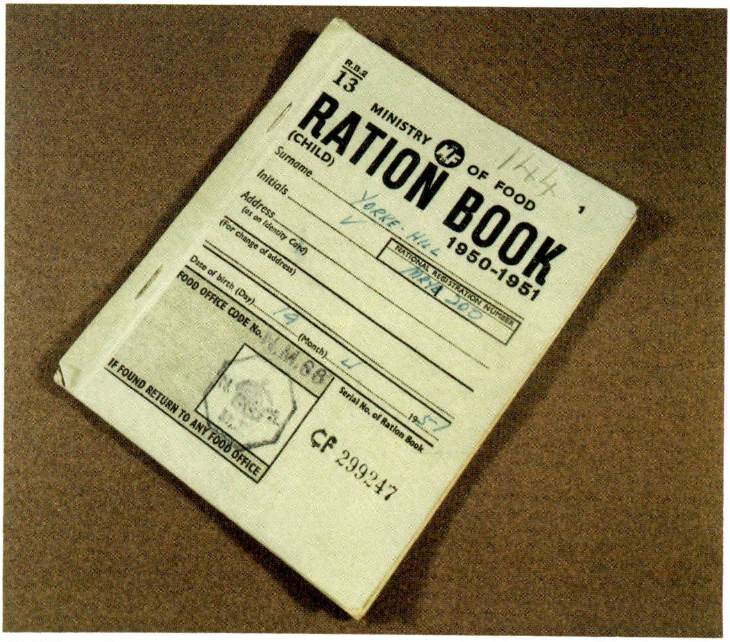

Child's ration book issued in 1951, eleven years after rationing began and three years before it ended.

would allow any money to be spent or issue licenses for any materials, and this consent was required as well as, not instead of, the consent of local authorities, which would be given or withheld on quite different grounds. No wonder Frederick Bandet found local builders unenthusiastic about putting up a factory for him.

In Hitchin, as we have seen, Bandet could count on support, although there were those who feared the effect of industrial development on the town's character. The central authorities – the 'gentlemen in Whitehall' – represented at the local level by 'the man from the Ministry' (a nice social distinction here) were biased against factory building. They had to contend with a shortage of almost everything, including labour and materials, and they would certainly have opposed his plan for an industrial estate if they had realised that it lay behind each of his applications for consent to a single project. He needed all his powers of diplomacy, all his patience, all his professional training, and much time for visits to Cambridge.

In the circumstances, reinforcing the cautious cast of Frederick Bandet's character, progress was bound to be small in scale and slow. The whole enterprise was governed by the availability of finance though not so much by the sums which Bandet could raise, as by the sums which the authorities would let him spend. So far as raising capital went, his credit in the locality was already good and he could borrow without difficulty. William Ainsley, the manager of the Midland Bank in Hitchin, offered an overdraft as soon as Bandet transferred his account from Baldock, and for longer term borrowing his accountants, Messrs Watts Knowles & Co of Letchworth, could find private individuals willing to offer £5,000, £10,000, or in one case £20,000.

Bandet's activities, however, were not restricted by his credit but by the law. A certain amount of money might be spent without a specific permit, but the limit of this 'free' expenditure, which varied from one year to another, was never higher than £1,000 and at one period was thrust down to £500. However, since the year in which the money might be spent was counted from 1st July, it was possible in a good year to spend as much as £2,000 during the best season for building –

PROFIT AND LOSS ACCOUNT for the two years ended 31st DECEMBER, 1952.

To Purchase and Sub-contracting		8399 – 10	By Sales and Work Done	563 1 9
,, Wages, etc.		1132 18 10	,, Rent Receivable	166 2 9
,, Rent, Rates and Insurances		617 6 4	,, Stock and Work in Progress,	
,, Light and Heat		75 19 5	31st December, 1952	12100 – –
,, Repairs and Renewals		355 18 6		
,, Car and Mixer Expenses		561 17 1		
,,Carriage and Transport		33 12 8		
,, Postage and Telephone		156 17 0		
,, Travel and Entertainment		39 1 4		
,, Printing, Stationery and Advertisements		213 2 10		
,, Bank Interest		367 2 9		
,, Loan Interest (Net)		132 16 3		
,, Loss on Sale of Plant		50 – –		
,, Sundry Expenses		160 3 2		
,, Audit Fee		17 10 –		
,, Depreciation:–				
Motor Vehicle	378 – –			
Plant and Machinery	60 7 1			
Fixtures and Fittings	1 – –	439 7 1		
,, Profit for period		439 7 1		
		76 10 –		
		£12829 4 6		£12829 4 6

The 1952 Profit and Loss Account and Balance Sheet of Erecta Hitchin Limited.

BALANCE SHEET as at 31st DECEMBER, 1952.

SHARE CAPITAL AUTHORISED & ISSUED			
100 Shares of £1 each fully paid			100 0 0
PROFIT AND LOSS ACCOUNT – General			
Profit for period			76 10 0
			176 10 0
LOAN ACCOUNTS			
F. Bandet	9605 0 0		
Less: Repaid during period	1830 0 0	7775 0 0	
E. Barker		730 0 0	
Mrs. Barker	350 0 0		
Less: Repaid during period	350 0 0	– – –	
E. Ray		3900 0 0	
Banley Ltd.	280 0 0		
Less: Repaid during period	194 1 0	85 19 0	
Hitchin Breeze Block Co. Ltd.	100 0 0		
Less: Repaid during period	100 0 0	– – –	
R. Bandet		300 0 0	12790 19 0
SUNDRY CREDITORS & ACCRUED CHARGES			1912 0 5
BANK OVERDRAFT (Secured by Mortgage)			5183 5 10
			£20062 15 3

FIXED ASSETS		
MOTOR VEHICLE at cost	1050 0 0	
Less: Depreciation to date	378 0 0	672 0 0
PLANT at cost	318 17 1	
Less: Depreciation to date	60 7 1	258 10 0
FIXTURES AND FITTINGS at cost	11 0 0	
Less: Depreciation to date	1 0 0	10 0 0
FREEHOLD PREMISES, WILBURY WAY, HITCHIN at cost		4000 0 0
LEASEHOLD PREMISES. WILBURY WAY, HITCHIN Expenditure to date at cost		600 0 0
		5540 10 0
CURRENT ASSETS		
F. BANDET: Current Account	1176 1 5	
HITCHIN BREEZE BLOCK CO. LTD. – Current Account	930 12 9	
SUNDRY DEBTORS	290 14 10	
STOCK & WORK IN PROGRESS as valued by a Director	12100 0 0	14497 9 0
PRELIMINARY EXPENSES at cost		24 16 3
		£20062 15 3

AUDITORS' REPORT TO THE MEMBERS OF ERECTA (HITCHIN) Limited.

We have obtained all the information and explanations which to the best of our knowledge and belief were necessary for the purposes of In our opinion proper books of account have been kept by the Company so far as appears from our examination of those books. We have examined the above Balance Sheet which is in agreement with the books of account. In our opinion and to the best of our information and according to the extractions given us, the said Balance Sheet gives the information required by the Companies Act, 1948 in the manner so required and exhibits a true and fair view of the state of the Company's affairs as at the 31st December, 1952 and the Profit and Loss Account gives a true and fair view of affairs for the two years ended on that date.

Letchworth,
3rd September, 1953.

Watts Knowles & Co.
Chartered Accountants

between, say, April and August. After that, any extra expenditure would need a supplementary licence from the regional office of the Ministry of Works in Cambridge, and if that was not forthcoming all work on the job would cease, perhaps for eighteen or twenty months.

To carry out his plans, Frederick Bandet set up two private companies. One, Hitchin Breeze Block Co. Limited, was incorporated on 23rd October 1951 to make breeze blocks which like so many other things at that time, were 'in short supply'. The other, with singular innocence, he called Erecta (Hitchin) Limited; a name which seemed to him to imply construction and also something positive, straightforward and upright – as indeed it also did in another sense from that which occurred to him. That did not strike him until, years later, he heard some secretaries giggling.

As scarcity at length began to give way to abundance, the importance of the breeze block company dwindled, and in the spring of 1955 it went out of production. Bandet then changed its name to Erecta Contractors Limited and it took on a wholly new activity. Through it land and materials were purchased, planning permission was obtained, staff were engaged, sub-contracts were arranged, and building work was carried out. As factories were completed and let, they were sold to Erecta (Hitchin) Limited, which thus became the first of Frederick Bandet's Investment Companies, and it is possible to discern the earliest outlines of today's Hunting Gate Group beginning to take shape.

These Investment Companies, of which Erecta (Hitchin) was the first, were and are of the first importance to Frederick Bandet. They were set up and are maintained to further the ultimate purpose of all his business activities, pursued with unwavering tenacity from their beginnings to the present day. That purpose is not primarily to make profits from sales of property but to create the most solid assets it is possible to own –buildings–as the guarantee of his own and his family's security far into the future.

Accordingly, since it was never the intention to make large profits from construction, the prices charged by the construction company to the Investment Companies were always on the low side of the average of the market. The consequences are apparent in the earliest accounts of Erecta (Hitchin) Limited, covering the fourteen months ending 31st December 1952, which also, incidentally, show how small Bandet's business was at that time. The balance sheet shows assets of £20,062 15s 3d*, of which £4,600 0s 0d represents freehold and leasehold premises in Wilbury Way and £12,100 0s 0d, stock and work in progress. The capital employed, apart from £100 in £1 shares, consists chiefly of loans to a total of £12,790 19s, of which £7,775 was due to F Bandet, and a bank overdraft of £5,183 5s 10d, secured by mortgage. The profit for the period is shown as £76 10s, emphasising that the purpose of Erecta (Hitchin) was not to make immediate profits but to create wealth in the shape of investments in bricks and mortar.

The company's Hitchin office was in a blue caravan deprived of its wheels and parked on concrete blocks among grazing cows at one end of Wilbury Way. It had two compartments, one for Frederick Bandet and the other for Albert Haley, and at Bandet's end no smoking was allowed. At the other end even his jibe 'Burn As You Earn' failed to extinguish Haley's pipe. Reproached some years later with the caravan's lack of facilities,

*roughly equivalent to £167,000 at today's prices

Ben Bates

The caravan used by Frederick Bandet and Albert Haley.

THE SPREADING OF 4444

HEAD OFFICE
Telephone:
Hitchin (04623) 4444

LONDON OFFICE
Telephone:
01-499 4444

PURLEY OFFICE
Telephone:
01-668 4444

SAN FRANCISCO OFFICE
Telephone:
(US Area Code 415) 392 4444

MENLO PARK OFFICE
Telephone:
(US Area Code 415) 327 4444

4444 THE COMPANY LOGO

The logo of the Hunting Gate Group, which has been evolved since 1972 in the company's own design office, incorporates the telephone number 4444 (see page opposite).

It was first displayed simply as the unadorned number (A).

In 1972 trowels were introduced (B), at first upright then (C) slanted.

Other designs were put forward, including one with telephone handsets (D), but after discussion it was rejected.

The fours were joined together in 1976, producing a strong, distinctive logo (E) which today appears on all stationery, brochures and advertising material (including boards on building sites) used by Group companies, thus emphasising the Group's essential unity.

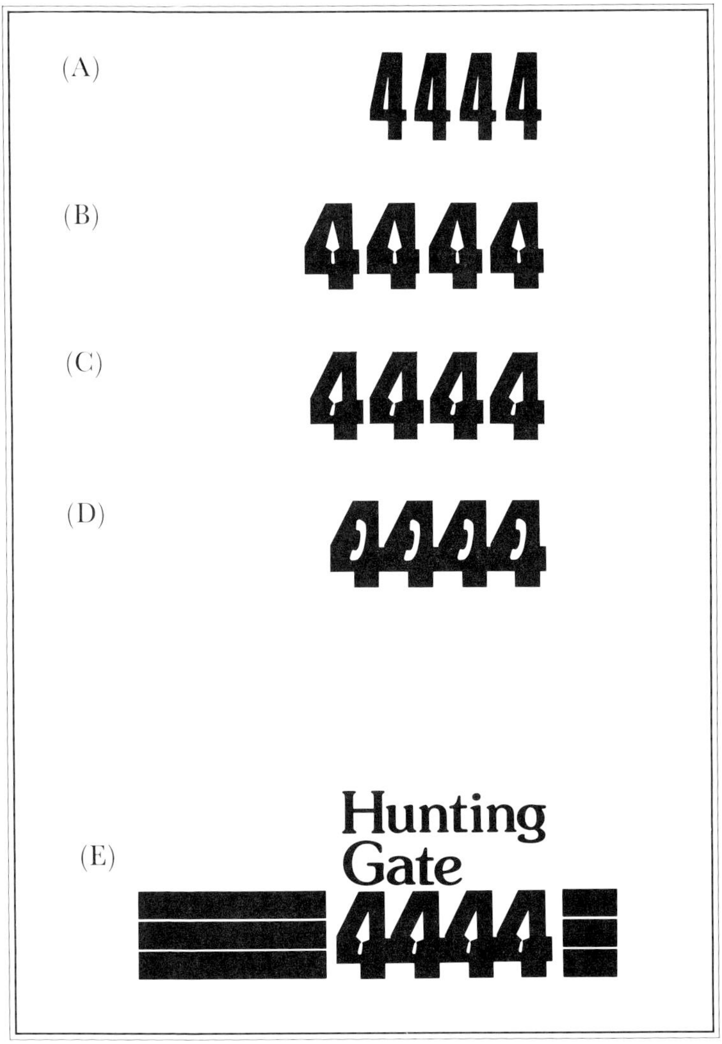
(A)
4444
(B)
4444
(C)
4444
(D)
4444
(E)
Hunting
Gate
4444

Bandet defended himself. It did not lack facilities, he said. All you had to do was to open the door, get on a bicycle, and pedal over to Albert Haley's house a few hundred yards away.

For the caravan's telephone Frederick Bandet went to considerable trouble in persuading the GPO to let him have an easily memorable number. He had to wait some months and then they assigned him Hitchin 4444. Since then telephone authorities elsewhere have been similarly co-operative, so that not only in Hitchin but in London and in California the number 4444 has come to mean first Erecta and later Hunting Gate. With the shape of a trowel inserted into each figure 4, the telephone number has developed into the Group's logotype.

The permanent staff of Erecta, in the fifties, was tiny. Albert Haley counted his service from 1946, though he did not come into the firm's full-time employment until 1959. Ben Bates and Peter Smyth, still with Hunting Gate Group in 1983, started in 1946 and 1959; both worked at anything that might be needed. The bulk of the building work was done by self-employed subcontractors – bricklayers in pairs with a labourer to mix mortar, carpenters, plumbers, and electricians. Apart from a car and a concrete-mixer, the firm owned virtually no plant.

Frederick Bandet in the early fifties was living quietly in the house he rented from John Ray. For a time his sister kept house for him, though Hitchin was not greatly to her taste, which is essentially metropolitan. Bandet spent little and took no holidays and, as long as building restrictions were severe, the service of his overdraft, before factories were let, gave him no anxiety. He had given up, he says, the intellectual and musical interests of his youth in Czecho-Slovakia, and in his reading he did not move much beyond the heavier newspapers and *The Economist*, all of which he read assiduously.

ERECTA (HITCHIN) LTD

The first brochure, written by Frederick Bandet in 1953.

As soon as factories were let, they produced income. By 1953 he had income from three factories in Wilbury Way, let to companies of the English Electric group for the development of guided missiles, and from one or two factories elsewhere. Getting a tenant of the standing of English Electric was a major achievement, and more were to follow. In an effort to attract them, Bandet produced his first publicity material; a ten-page brochure about 7½ inches by 5 inches written by himself and illustrated with pictures of factories which he had already put up on the Hitchin Industrial Estate. It was aimed chiefly at employers in the light engineering and electrical industries and it tells us a good deal, directly and by implication, about the hopeful and expansive atmosphere of the early nineteen-fifties.

'Few towns', says the brochure, 'in the outer country ring of

London, combine the advantages which Hitchin offers to the industrialist. It is conveniently near London, yet well outside the congested suburban approach roads. In a good open position, it has a labour population which at present works largely outside the town.' This fact 'is much lamented in local circles', and a letter to the Hertfordshire Express is quoted in which the writer says that more factories 'would add greatly to the prosperity of Hitchin'.

The brochure next points out, for no very obvious reason, 'that there are no unemployed, or rather that the limited number of persons on the books of the labour exchanges cannot, in these days, be taken to prove anything about the disposition of engineering and other labour in Hitchin and the surrounding industrial centres of Letchworth, Stevenage and Luton.' What can, apparently, be proved is that people in Hitchin 'naturally prefer to work, if possible, near their homes . . . They greatly value the convenience of lunch at home and the saving in ever-increasing fares, although the costs of these are ultimately borne by the employer and reflected in less competitive products.' Elsewhere, the brochure mentions that there is plenty of council housing 'within easy cycling distance'. The day of the factory worker's car had not quite arrived.

Hoping, no doubt, to indicate that skilled labour was plentiful, the brochure pointed out that the engineering and electrical industries were strongly represented in the area. That might be a doubtful advantage. What if rival employers poached each other's men? The brochure is reassuring: 'Nevertheless, a man trained locally in a special field would not find employment in a rival concern as easily as, say, in London.'

In spite of the busy, optimistic tone of this brochure, the permitted level of building activity in the early fifties was still

An effective way of national advertising.

THE INDUSTRY BUILDERS

If all building projects were merely a question of construction, industrialists would have very few headaches.

But they are not. At Hunting Gate we appreciate this and our team of development and building specialists includes planning experts, architects, surveyors, building engineers, financiers and lawyers all working under our own roof to ensure that we are prepared for every eventuality.

We develop our clients sites, our own sites or seek out a specific site to meet a client's requirements.

We handle complete individual 'design and build' projects from initial planning, through financing to construction – and we complete on target.

We pioneered industrial estate partnership schemes with local authorities.

In the past year, these are just a few of Britain's foremost companies who took advantage of our comprehensive service –

- BOC Limited
- Engineering Laboratory Equipment Ltd.
- The Goodyear Tyre and Rubber Company (Gt. Britain) Ltd.
- Regma (UK) Ltd.

For our corporate brochure please contact:

4444

Hunting Gate Group
– More Than Builders

Hunting Gate
Hitchin
Herts SG4 0TB
Telephone: (0462) 4444
Telex: 82444

One of the first national advertisements.

too low to keep Frederick Bandet fully occupied. Family connections provided him with the extra activity he needed. In 1951 Ellie Bandet married Eric Walter Barker, who had also come to England from Czecho-Slovakia; from a town near Troppau called Mährisch Ostrau. He ran a successful business, together with his wife, importing high-class chocolates and confectionery from the Continent, especially Germany, Austria and Switzerland. They had an office in Ludgate Hill in the City. Bandet, under-employed, went into the business with them, and for some years he divided his activities between property in Hitchin and confectionery in London. The pamphlet quoted above gives the address of Erecta (Hitchin) Limited as 34/40 Ludgate Hill.

He had always kept a foothold in London: at first a furnished room and then, between 1949 and 1956, a mansion-flat in Torrington Place, WC1, near University College Hospital. Then a small advertisement in the *Evening Standard* attracted his attention. He followed it up and found that it had been put in by Lady Drummond whose husband, Air Vice Marshal Sir Peter Drummond, had died in 1945 aged scarcely more than fifty. Lady Drummond was living in Campden Hill Gate, a large block of flats built in the thirties in Duchess of Bedford's Walk, Kensington, near Holland Park, but she was looking for something smaller. Bandet had been looking for some time for a flat near a park and Lady Drummond's was just what he wanted. He called on Lady Drummond on the evening of the day when the advertisement appeared and very quickly agreed to buy her lease.

Bandet knew Campden Hill Gate and its neighbourhood well. Duchess of Bedford's Walk was named after the Dowager Duchess of the sixth duke. She lived at one time in Bedford

Mr. & Mrs. Barker's wedding 1951.

Lodge (later Argyll Lodge) nearby. She was a great lady in the tradition of the eighteenth century rather than the nineteenth, lively and unconventional. Her entertainments, said the *Illustrated London News* in July, 1846 'possess all that delightful sociality which cannot fail to render them extremely popular among the high and noble class for whose enjoyment they are especially designed.'

The land south of Campden Hill, including the site of Campden Hill Gate, belonged long ago to the Phillimores of Gloucestershire. In 1779 William Phillimore inherited his great-grandfather's estate and began to develop it in the manner of the Grosvenors and other great London landowners. As the name 'Phillimore Gardens' indicates, he started extensive speculative building along Kensington High Street and in the streets near Duchess of Bedford's Walk. It was an appropriate place for a rising property developer such as Frederick Bandet to put down roots.

In Holland Park had stood Holland House, a Jacobean mansion which came into the possession of the third Lord Holland (1773-1840). In 1797 he married Elizabeth Vassall (1770-1845) three days after her husband, Sir Godfrey Webster, divorced her for adultery. Until she died she entertained largely, brilliantly and scandalously, making Holland House a political and cultural centre for Whig aristocrats distinguished by the height of their social standing, the depth of their radicalism, and their total disregard for Victorian notions of propriety.

Holland House was destroyed by German bombs, which left no more than a fragment standing. Holland Park, ironically, was bought for £2 million in 1951 by the Labour-controlled LCC, representing a brand of radicalism different indeed from that of Lord and Lady Holland. Frederick Bandet found solitary

From the original drawing by the architect, Mr. John D. Coleridge, which illustrated the first prospectus issued in 1932 and is kindly made available by Chestertons.

CAMPDEN HILL GATE

FETE CHAMPETRE AT BEDFORD LODGE

BEDFORD LODGE, the beautiful villa residence of the Duchess (Dowager) of Bedford, at Campden Hill, has obtained a high degree of celebrity among fashionable circles during the last few years, from the delightful fêtes, of which it is annually the scene.

Unlike the somewhat formal gatherings of the aristocracy which we are occasionally called upon to notice, the Duchess of Bedford's *réunions* possess all that delightful sociality which cannot fail to render them extremely popular among the high and noble class for whose enjoyment they are especially designed.

At Bedford Lodge, during the London season, not only are all the most distinguished members of the aristocracy weekly visitants and participators in the hospitality of the noble hostess; but Royalty itself, in the person of the Princes and Princesses of the Blood Royal, seldom omits the opportunity of joining the festive scene.

One peculiarity attending the Duchess of Bedrord's *fêtes* is, that her Grace issues no formal invitations. A passing word from the noble hostess, or an announcement in the *Morning Post*, to the effect that her Grace's *fêtes* will commence on a particular date, is sufficient to insure the presence of all the leading members of the fashionable world at Bedford Lodge on the appointed day.

Another feature is the opportunity of enjoyment which her Grace affords to the juvenile members of the aristocracy. In the grounds of her Grace's villa, the youthful scions of the nobility meet; and here, probably, lay the foundation of friendships which, in after years, ripen into attachments of a closer and dearer nature.

The above sketch was taken on the 10th instant, upon the occasion of his Highness Ibrahim Pacha, attended by the members of his suite, honouring the Duchess with his presence. His Highness was evidently greatly amused by the scene the gardens presented. The air of freedom and enjoyment everywhere prevailing appeared to have influence on the Pacha's usually somewhat reserved temperament; and, in a very short time after his introduction, he engaged in earnest conversation with the Duke of Cambridge, Viscount Lascelles, and several other noblemen.

A fête in the grounds of Bedford Lodge now occupied by Campden Hill Gate. Reproduced from *Illustrated London News*, 20th July, 1846, by courtesy of The Royal Borough of Kensington and Chelsea Libraries.

The Phillimore Estate, Kensington in 1872, showing the site North of Duchess of Bedford's Walk on which Campden Hill Gate was built 60 years later. Plan reproduced by courtesy of The Royal Borough of Kensington and Chelsea Libraries.

Mrs. Joyce Cannings in 1982

walks in Holland Park far more conducive to creative thought than a seat behind a desk.

After Bandet bought the lease of 8 Campden Hill Gate he remained friendly with Lady Drummond and her family. He became friendly also with the manager of the property company who owned the block, Richard Barter. Barter offered a similar flat to the Barkers, and in the late fifties they moved into Campden Hill Gate as well. In his own flat, Bandet set up an office to deal with his property interests, and it appears as the address of Erecta Limited in one of his early brochures, though for some time he went on spending his afternoons in the City. In May 1958 he engaged a secretary, Mrs Joyce Cannings, for his office in Campden Hill Gate. She worked for him there until he left for California in 1976. Her counterpart in the Hitchin office, from 1968 to 1976, was Mary Ridehalgh.

In 1958 Frederick Bandet passed his forty-fifth birthday. Rather less than twenty years earlier, he had undergone an ordeal, alone in a foreign country, which nothing but his innate quality of dour strength had enabled him to survive. He had done much more than survive. He had prospered. Even more than that, perhaps, he had established himself in alien surroundings: the world of the North Atlantic, far removed in distance and in culture from his native Central Europe.

In 1958, after due deliberation, as is his way, Frederick Bandet married. His bride was Dorothy-Rose Harper, who came from a family background far removed from his own. Her father, G.C. Harper, was educated in the heart of the English 'Establishment' at Shrewsbury School and Christ Church, 'The House', of all the Oxford colleges the most aloof and aristocratic, not to

say arrogant. His career, unconventional but distinguished, began as a traffic apprentice with the London & North Eastern Railway and ended as one of Her Majesty's Inspectors of Schools (Divisional Inspector for Metropolitan London). He married as his first wife a French woman, Mrs Bandet's mother, and he is an Officer of the French Academy.

Mrs Bandet herself went to Oxford to read Modern Languages. She has preferred to keep her distance from her husband's business, taking little part in business entertaining and in no way asserting her position as the founder's wife. Mr and Mrs Bandet set up house in Campden Hill Gate. Number 8 was sold and two flats, 20 and 21, were linked to provide a dwelling place and a separate, self-contained office.

Between 1960 and 1963 three children were born: Gina, (Regina), Isabel and Henry. Bandet thenceforward was not building the business for himself alone, but for the next generation of his family and for generations yet to come. His patriarchal instinct is very strong. *Vita nova in aedificiis novis* – some people do not understand it, but Frederick Bandet means it.

Mrs. Dorothy-Rose Bandet, 1983.

Chapter Five

THE SIXTIES

The Sixties

GREAT Britain in the sixties, along with other industrial nations, was riding the crest of the greatest and longest boom the world has known; twenty-five years of rapid, widespread economic growth based on technical innovation and plentiful oil at pre-OPEC prices, giving a corresponding increase in world trade. In the countries of the OECD and Japan, industrial production more than doubled between 1948 and 1963 and then increased by nearly 50% between 1963 and 1970. Over the same period the value of exports of manufactures from eleven countries rose by more than 700%, from $18.6 billion to nearly $155 billion, and these were figures not yet grossly distorted by inflation.

In Great Britain, in spite of the prevailing prosperity, there had for many years been signs of grave economic *malaise*, giving rise to persistent anxiety about the balance of payments and erupting periodically in 'sterling crises', which simply meant that foreigners understood the truth about Britain more clearly than most of the British chose to do. Nothing resolute was done, but Ministers still liked to believe that they were 'managing the economy', and whenever it became more than usually evident that they were not, they used phrases like 'fine tuning', 'a touch on the tiller', and 'steady as she goes'. On a superficial view, everything was going well enough. Unemployment was low, material prosperity was high, the costs of the Welfare State did not seem to be insupportable, and for many people life was increasingly cosy and by no means over-strenuous.

In these agreeable circumstances many luxuries could be permitted, not least a withering onslaught, delivered with the aid of some of the most brilliant artistic talent that television, the theatre, the cinema and literature could attract, upon the whole social, political and moral framework of the State. This assault,

Leaving *SS Canberra* after a Mediterranean Cruise, 1960.

which had long been building up, found a receptive audience and gained a great deal of support in the schools and universities. Nothing escaped. The most respected national institutions, every manifestation of authority, traditional standards of conduct and morality were all held up to hatred, ridicule – especially ridicule – and contempt. A deluge of destructive criticism, with very little admixture of constructive thought, swept through the sixties, inducing a strange national mood of self-abasement and giggling frivolity. The retreat from Empire, begun as a slow march in 1947, quickened during the sixties to the pace of an undignified and guilt-ridden scramble, and with the decline of British power Great Britain became, to the horror of some and the delight of others, an acknowledged leader of the 'Swinging Sixties'. As the Union Flag came down, the mini-skirt went up.

Economic growth, during the long post-war boom, came to seem like a law of nature, and a rising standard of living appeared to be one of the rights of man. The achievement of both became a prime objective of high policy: in Germany and Japan it was strikingly successful. In Great Britain the rate of growth, at 2½ per cent a year or so, was probably as great as at any time in the nation's history, and as for standards of living, Harold MacMillan, when Prime Minister, was certainly right when he inelegantly told people they 'had never had it so good', but comparison with the two ex-enemies was not flattering.

The period of the boom was also a period of continuous international political instability and tension, dominated by the mutual hostility and suspicion of the alliances led by Russia on the one hand and by the USA on the other, and by the power vacuum left by the collapse of the great colonial empires, the British Empire above all. International discord, by encouraging industrial activity and technological advance, must have done a great deal to foster economic growth. Prosperity often grows out of the barrel of a gun.

In the later fifties, scarcity in all departments of the national life at last gave way to plenty. Wartime controls, except exchange control, had disappeared by 1955, and among them the controls which had hampered Frederick Bandet's first efforts in building. At the same time there was a buoyant demand for factory space, inspired by confidence that although from time to time there might be minor recessions – as there were – yet in the long run growth would be part of the natural order.

The danger of inflation was not yet taken so seriously as to undermine all confidence in the future value of money. Insurance companies in the sixties were prepared to lend for terms of twenty or thirty years at rates of interest – eight, nine, perhaps even eleven per cent – which afterwards came to seem low, and so long as factory rents at first letting could be negotiated so as to cover mortgage interest, they could be adjusted in the periodical rent reviews to do a good deal more. It is a mark of the generally low rate of inflation that rent reviews, in a twenty-one year lease, were usually arranged to take place every seven years, not, as later, every three.

With controls abolished and materials no longer scarce, with demand strong and long-term finance available at manageable interest rates, property developers flourished; among them, Frederick Bandet. In 1961 he withdrew from partnership with his sister and brother-in-law – like other autocrats, he does not relish partnership – and set himself free to devote his whole time to his property interests.

These interests, in the early sixties, were still wholly confined to the Hitchin Industrial Estate, but the centre of the property world – the head offices of large firms of chartered surveyors and of desirable tenants – was in London. Frederick Bandet therefore spent part of his time in his London flat near Holland Park, where Mrs Cannings worked; part in Hitchin. In Hitchin he had a bungalow, Fir Tree Cottage. It was not grand, but then grandeur, as distinct from comfortable opulence, was not then and is not now part of Frederick Bandet's way of life.

With the help of Mrs Cannings as his secretary in London and of Albert Haley as his building manager in Hitchin, but with hardly any other permanent employees except Ben Bates, Frederick Bandet worked along Wilbury Way, building and letting. Up to 1964 he had completed over a dozen factories of one or two storeys, some with high, impressive frontages. The largest, of about 28,000 square feet, was put up for the company which became International Computers Limited and the aim was always, so far as possible, to find first-class public companies or their equivalent as tenants. The land was originally taken mainly on ground leases from the Wallace family who, through Buryfield Estates, owned the freehold. In 1971, Bandet bought Buryfield Estates Limited, so that the freehold passed to him.

In 1961 Bandet laid out a new estate road eastwards at right angles to Wilbury Way. On the boundary of the estate, it was said, there had once been a gate used by riders to hounds. The surroundings of the estate on all sides, except that towards Hitchin, were thoroughly rural, as in 1983 they still are, and in consultation with Anthony King, Surveyor to Hitchin UDC, Frederick Bandet decided to play up that aspect of his property. He called the new road Hunting Gate. Did Dan Archer, perhaps, once pass that way?

Beside his first building in Hunting Gate was a two-storey

The development of the Hitchin Industrial Estate 1956-1974.

Originally let to Ryman Group Limited. 1967. Offices and warehousing at Woolmer Green, Hertfordshire.

These offices and factory units in Wilbury Way were built to Frederick Bandet's own design. Professional opinion at the time was against the addition of upper floors.

A nearly completed building now occupied by Rona Laboratories, Cadwell Lane, Hitchin, 1968.

28,200 sq.ft. office building, Wilbury Way, originally let to Control Dataset. Built 1966.

Ceremonial opening of the Panel Fabrication factory at Icknield Way, Baldock by Mrs. Hoeg, wife of the Chairman of Baldock UDC, with Gina Bandet handing over the scissors. 1969.

factory let to an engineering firm which only used the ground floor. In 1963, Frederick Bandet decided to exchange the eccentric informality of the caravan amongst the cows for a suite of offices better suited to the management of a business which by then must have had assets of a market value running well into six figures and perhaps towards seven. He moved himself into one office, Albert Haley into another, on the engineering company's unused upper floor, with a secretary to work for both of them. For a rising property magnate, his ideas of office staff and accommodation could scarcely be called extravagant.

Fred Hillyard is a highly skilled joiner who works for Hunting Gate today, as he has done since 1965. At that time, although he was living in Hitchin, he had never heard of the Erecta business until he came to apply for a job with it. It was so local an affair that it was not even known from one end of the town to the other. Great changes, however, were by then beginning, preparing the way, ultimately, for great expansion.

First, the financial basis of Erecta's operations had to be reinforced. In 1964 Frederick Bandet, accompanied by Keith Guyton, for many years his accountant and financial adviser, went to a meeting in London with representatives of Sun Life of Canada, in order to discuss a proposal for a mortgage: £100,000 at seven per cent repayable over thirty years. The meeting opened badly, for in Canada they had not been impressed by the strength of Erecta's balance sheet. During the discussion Guyton, to Bandet's horror, offered to go to Canada, at Sun Life's expense, and teach them how to read it. Its strength lay in what was *not* included, namely, the value of the property shown as assets, which was based on their cost to Erecta, not on their likely value in the market. Guyton's tactics apparently worked. Within a few days Sun Life accepted the proposal. He did not go to Canada.

The proposition included a five year 'holiday' from repayment of the principal. Taken with the money he could borrow on overdraft from the Midland Bank, it gave Frederick Bandet the working capital he needed for more ambitious expansion. The prospect of expansion presented him, for the first time in his career, with the necessity of finding capable managers. Frederick Bandet and Albert Haley, that curiously assorted duo, could no longer run Erecta on their own. Nor would Haley be running anything for very much longer, for by 1964 he was in sight of retirement.

Bandet would very much like to have employed Julian Vivian, an estate agent considerably younger than himself who had set up in business in 1952 and had first been engaged by Frederick Bandet about a year later in the letting of a small factory in Wilbury Way. From that early contact, tinged at first on Vivian's side with slight suspicion of the foreigner, a business relationship developed which eventually merged with friendship – Frederick Bandet stood godfather in 1964 to Vivian's son – founded on mutual respect and trust.

In spite of warm personal regard, Vivian steadily refused Bandet's offers, even when one of them was accompanied by a draft agreement in which Vivian was invited to insert the salary. Vivian felt very strongly that his abilities lay in working as an agent, not as a principal; that his most promising future lay in that direction; and that it was in that capacity he could best serve Frederick Bandet, not as a salaried employee. Moreover, he knew that Bandet as an employer would be generous, but very demanding. 'Instead of coming to you myself,' said Vivian, 'I will find you someone'. He drafted an advertisement which

The Westbury

One bedroom terraced house

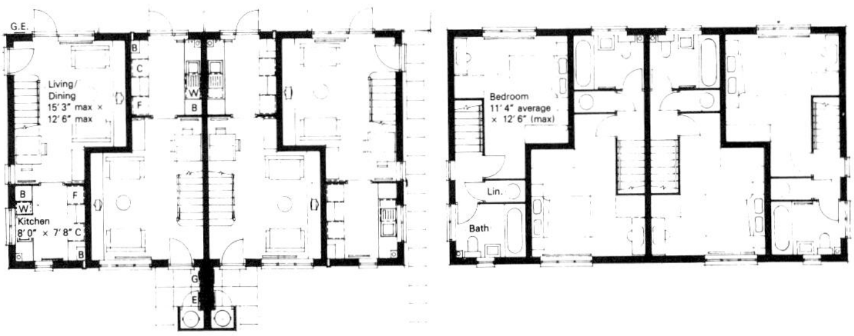

Architect's illustration plus plans of the 'Westbury' one bedroom starter home.

Three-bedroom detached houses at Ickleford, 1966.

appeared in the *Estates Gazette*.

Among those who replied was D. B. Moore, then in his mid-thirties. Moore had qualified as an architect from the Architectural Association's school but, against the rules of his profession as they were then drawn (they have since been altered), he had gone into business, and when he applied for the job Bandet was offering, he was working for a firm of property developers as a manager chiefly concerned with housing. He was gregarious and out-going; a rose-grower of some note; a skilled joiner; a good amateur musician, married to a professional pianist. In business he had the instincts of an *entrepreneur* and large ambitions, but he was without capital, and he was looking for an opportunity to share the equity of a growing business. This opportunity the position at Hunting Gate appeared to offer.

Frederick Bandet evidently recognised in David Moore talents complementary to his own, and after a very short acquaintance he engaged him. 'He brought with him', said Bandet in 1971, 'tremendous enthusiasm, a *joie de vivre* and a lot of pressure and vibration. Things began to happen: we straightaway launched the building company, Hunting Gate Homes.'

When he engaged Moore, Bandet was preparing, with his usual deliberate caution – one step at a time, each carefully tested – to move into housing. At Ickleford, a mile or two northward of Hitchin, he had bought a site for twelve houses, and for this site David Moore designed three-bedroom detached houses typical of their £4,000 price and period, with wood-block floors, central heating, picture windows, and a tile-hung facade. On other sites Hunting Gate put up three-storey 'town houses' – the recently-coined synonym for 'terrace houses' – and three and four bedroom houses both detached and semi-detached, at prices ranging up to £6,000. They were attractive houses, well finished and well fitted, set in carefully 'landscaped' surroundings. As the publicity material put it: 'The small number of town houses to be built will offer a completely new standard of living', and the same might have been said, without indecent exaggeration, of the other houses too.

They were houses for people on the way up, neatly encapsulated, again, in publicity material for the town houses: 'Within one basic design the needs of a business couple requiring a well fitted and spacious home for entertaining, and the large family having need of 4 bedrooms and 2 bathrooms, can both be met.' 'Business couples' would value nearby amenities, such as Letchworth Hall Hotel and Golf Course. The large family would not only need bedrooms and bathrooms, but schools. Both parties in the 'business couple' would need to travel to work, and transport would be needed for children going to school and wives going shopping. The houses were on land bought with all these needs in mind, and publicity material makes a point of bus services, access to main roads, and railway connections to London – 'King's Cross in a little over 40 minutes by train.' They were houses for busy, ambitious, mobile people.

The move into housing was significant for two reasons. First it carried Frederick Bandet, for the first time, outside the boundaries of the Hitchin Industrial Estate. Secondly, it carried him, again for the first time, into a deliberate policy of building for sale, not for letting. The houses, unlike factories, were to be sold to new owners, not let to tenants. The units would be much smaller, but the turnover, it was to be hoped, much faster, and the proceeds would provide a useful flow of cash which could be directed into the industrial side of the business, which would remain larger and more important than housing.

With the engagement of David Moore, Frederick Bandet launched his policy, on which he places strong emphasis, of building up within the business a staff of professionally qualified specialists, thus very greatly reducing his need to go to independent firms and individuals for professional advice and services. The advantages and drawbacks of this policy are discussed, from the firm's point of view, in Chapter One. There is no doubt that its origins, which concern us here, are to be found in Frederick Bandet's personality, in his self-confidence, in his determination, and in his insistence on keeping every aspect of his business, as far as possible, under his own control. All his natural tendencies were reinforced by his experience with the architect whom he consulted about the building of his first factory: an experience which made a deep impression on his mind and, no doubt, gave him a rational justification for an instinctive attitude.

His method, generally speaking, has been to pick his men young and relatively inexperienced but over-qualified for the position to be filled. Then, on the principle 'Do what you're good at', he has allowed them scope to develop their abilities not only in their own specialities but also, if they have shown aptitude, in wider fields as well. Thus when he went into housing, he set up Hunting Gate Homes to handle it, providing scope for the exercise of David Moore's profession, though scarcely enough to keep him fully occupied. With Frederick Bandet's entire goodwill, Moore began to move towards general management.

Frederick Bandet himself, as the business grew, distanced himself from the decision-making process. A General, he says, may be forty or fifty miles from the battlefront, and he has a preference for letting proposals come to him for consideration – usually in the direction of caution – rather than handing decisions down. If this style of management has sometimes made it appear that he was ready to surrender control, or at least to share it, then appearances have been deceptive. Nor would it be safe to deduce that he is either afraid or incapable of decision-making.

In 1966 Albert Haley retired. For twenty years he had served, in effect, as Frederick Bandet's building manager, and he represented an older tradition in the building industry than that followed by the younger men whom Bandet was now beginning to recruit. Of Haley's native ability and grasp of practicalities there never seems to have been any doubt, but he never had any formal training in any trade or profession and he was never called upon to operate outside a rather limited sphere. Would he have felt at home in the management of a business as large, as diversified and as sophisticated, especially in financial matters, as Hunting Gate now showed signs of becoming?

Just before Haley went, Frederick Bandet brought two young men of the new model into the business. One, a quantity surveyor, moved on in 1974. The other was Eric Howlett, who had spent his whole career, apart from a couple of years in the Royal Engineers, in the building industry, latterly as a technical representative with Concrete Limited (Bison), which he joined in 1956.

A buoyant, forceful personality, expert knowledge, total devotion to the job in hand at any hour of the day or night established Eric Howlett firmly in his customers' esteem, and among his customers, in the early sixties, was Frederick Bandet, who formed a habit of getting Howlett to call on him at Campden Hill Gate to discuss work in progress. After about a couple of years of this kind of acquaintance Bandet, beginning to seek a replacement for Haley, decided he wanted Howlett, and just after Christmas 1965 he had a series of conversations with him, also at Campden Hill Gate.

Howlett, whose future at Bison looked bright, was not easily persuaded to join a smaller business, but Bandet, following his usual practice, offered attractive terms and in May 1966 he had his way. Howlett left the outskirts of London to take up an appointment as Building Manager with Hunting Gate. Bandet, characteristically, was engaging him not so much for what he was as for what, in Bandet's opinion, he might become. He described the job he was offering in very simple terms – 'You just do everything'.

When Frederick Bandet engaged Eric Howlett he engaged a thoroughly practical builder who was young enough to expand his technical competence as Hunting Gate expanded. He did not engage a property developer. For success in that occupation – as for success in most of the activities of the market place – vocational training is not enough. The essential ingredient is an inborn commercial instinct, including shrewd judgement

13th May 1966. Albert Haley retires after twenty years' service with Frederick Bandet.

of possibilities and of people. Experience may refine and perhaps intensify that instinct, but nothing will instil it if it is not there. Frederick Bandet himself acquired such technical knowldge as he needed by reading and by intelligent attendance upon experts, Albert Haley and Eric Howlett prominent among them, but this course of self-education on its own would never have carried Hunting Gate to success.

Among the most valuable powers conferred by the commercial instinct upon those who have it is the ability to recognise it in potential employees, regardless of any formal qualifications they may or may not possess. Frederick Bandet displayed this ability, it would appear, when he hired a young man called Danny Desmond in 1968.

Desmond, born in 1940, was a trader from his schooldays, which may be what led him into the property business. He began his career with a London firm of chartered surveyors, Jackson Stops & Staff, but he came to Hunting Gate from a firm of estate agents, Thorne Reeks, in Luton. He made an approach, about 1965, by writing to ask whether Hunting Gate needed anyone like him. The reply, which came from David Moore, said they didn't.

In 1967 Desmond saw an advertisement inserted by Hunting Gate in the local press for a building surveyor. He had no formal qualifications, but he applied, and this time David Moore was sufficiently impressed to see him several times. At the last interview Frederick Bandet was present as well, dressed casually in an open-necked shirt.

Desmond must have conveyed a businesslike impression, for he was taken on as a land negotiator. His job involved letting space on the industrial side of the business and acquiring sites for residential development, and he very quickly found himself concerned with house sales as well. There was no legal department and before long he was negotiating leases. If there were departures from the standard form, he would consult Frederick Bandet who, following his custom, would ring Desmond almost every evening, weekends included, to discuss what was going on.

As steel is to the shipbuilder, as flour is to the baker, so land is to the property developer. It is his indispensable raw material. Eric Howlett once suggested to Frederick Bandet that he might make a quick profit by selling a piece of land he had just bought. 'Look', Bandet replied, 'have you ever heard of a tailor selling cloth? He'll sell you a suit, but he doesn't sell you cloth – somebody else does that.' In appointing a young man from a Luton estate agent as a land negotiator, Frederick Bandet had appointed him to an activity which potentially carried the key to the success or failure of the business; a point which Desmond, as well as Bandet, was perfectly capable of appreciating.

In 1968, Frederick Bandet at last bought himself a house appropriate to his wealth and standing. Gosmore Hill, a few miles South of Hitchin, was not very attractive to look at, having been built, probably in the twenties, in a somewhat arid version of Stockbroker Tudor but it stood on a hillside with superb views, and it was secluded, with a lodge for resident staff and in about ten acres of ground, to which Bandet later added ten more, and a couple of bungalows.

The house was enlarged and improved to Eric Howlett's designs. So were the gardens. In the very cold November of 1968 Eric Howlett arrived on the site, together with two caterpillar tractors, a Michigan four-wheel-drive shovel, and fourteen lorries for carrying soil. Hedges were uprooted and replanted and the slope in front of the house was transformed into two lawns. Later, after Frederick Bandet bought the extra land, pleasant walks were created for the evening, illuminated by electric lights. Here, in an avenue of pine trees, Bandet had his 'Carpet Walk', where pine needles spread a soft carpet underfoot. As in Holland Park, he found solitary walking conducive to creative thought.

In the grounds of Gosmore, every summer from 1969 to 1975, Frederick Bandet would entertain his employees at a garden party. These parties developed a boisterous geniality symbolised by a pool, twelve feet square and four feet deep, built in the early years by Eric Howlett from plywood lined with polythene. Perched over the water astride a greasy pole, members of the staff were encouraged to engage in pillow-fights with senior executives: the results were predictable. The contests became traditional and in the later years were transferred to a small permanent swimming pool.

Apart from this licensed anarchy, the parties were aimed particularly at employees' children. After their parents had *quite* finished they were free to take over the swimming pool: besides that, a miniature fun-fair was set up for the day. A garden tractor towed the small ones round the grounds in a trailer. Boys of twelve to fourteen could show off as racing drivers in a go-kart. In some years there were donkey rides: in one, a relay race round a specially built obstacle course.

Staff parties are a normal feature of business life. They are notoriously difficult to assess. How far is the jollity spontaneous? How far is it politic? So far as it is possible for an outsider to judge, the success of the parties at Gosmore was genuine and unforced, contributing positively to the quality of life within Hunting Gate. They came to an end after Bandet left for California in 1976.

Gosmore Hill, Frederick Bandet's house in Hertfordshire.

The house was a source of great satisfaction to Bandet; less so to his wife, who preferred London. The children liked the country and spent many weekends at Gosmore, and as much of their holidays as they could. Frederick Bandet would be there from Tuesday morning until Friday afternoon, well looked after by his housekeeper, Mrs Farr. He would go back to London for weekends when the rest of his family were at Campden Hill Gate. Successful English business men for centuries have aspired to the life of a country gentleman, and Bandet followed in that tradition. He was striking roots deep into Hitchin and its neighbourhood, from the soil of which his success had sprung, in whose soil his security was founded.

By the time Frederick Bandet came to compose a Chairman's Statement to go with the Report and Accounts of the Hunting Gate Group – the name had just been adopted – for 1972, he could survey a business which had been growing very rapidly during the previous ten years and which already displayed the essential characteristics of the Hunting Gate Group of ten years later.

Figures to illustrate the growth of the Group are not readily available for the years before 1969-70, but between that year and the year 1971-72 the value of house sales went up by 193 per cent to £1,866,000; the gross rental income from industrial and office investment properties rose by 97 per cent to £347,000; and the Group net profit before tax, but after depreciation, increased by 357 per cent to £277,600.

The Hunting Gate Group in 1972 consisted of two operating companies – one for construction, another for residential development – and of Investment Companies, of which at the time there were nine. At the head of the Group, as Chairman and Managing Director, was Frederick Bandet. David Moore stood alongside him as Joint Managing Director. Danny Desmond and Eric Howlett, also, were both on the Board, Desmond 'in charge of property transactions generally' and Howlett 'responsible for non-residential construction and all structural engineering aspects of building work, road construction etc.'. Ronald Howman, the quantity surveyor mentioned earlier, was House Building Director. Keith Guyton, as Bandet's principal financial adviser, had a non-executive seat on the Board, but Bandet by this time was also taking advice from the London accountancy firm of Stoy Hayward & Co., a mark of the growing size and complexity of the Group's financial affairs. A senior partner, Alfred Davies, who attended Hunting Gate's Board meetings as Bandet's personal adviser, introduced him to Jeremy Raisman of Jaques & Co. (later Jaques & Lewis) of Gray's Inn, and to John Button of Ansbachers, the merchant bankers.

In that same year, 1972, Raisman became Bandet's personal legal adviser and, shortly afterwards, corporate solicitor to Hunting Gate Group and to all the Investment Companies. He was also later appointed one of the trustees of all Bandet's family trusts, a position which he held until the trusts' change of residence to America in 1981. Raisman and his partner Christopher Sly, a tax expert, have been involved in virtually all the many complex transactions that have taken place over more than ten years.

Below the level of the Board, Frederick Bandet's policy of employing professional people was by 1972 very evident. There were more than two dozen architects, solicitors, chartered surveyors, accountants and draftsmen. That, said the Annual Report, was 'probably the highest number of professional people for a company of its size in the property development and construction industry.' They certainly provided an impressively wide range of services.

Frederick Bandet kept the ownership and therefore the control of the Group which he had founded firmly in his own hands and the hands of his family trusts, but he had begun to reward his most senior employees with participation as well as handsome salaries and other benefits. The Annual Report for 1972 gives a list of shareholders in the various companies of the Group. As well as the names of Bandet himself and his wife, the names of Moore, Desmond, Howman and Howlett appear, in that order, and Keith Guyton also had a holding. The sizes of the Directors' holdings are not indicated, but at this time they were small in relation to Bandet's own, though no doubt large enough to whet the appetite for more.

The activities of the business, though still fairly heavily concentrated within twenty miles or so of Hitchin, were beginning to spread much further afield, even as far as Andover in Hampshire. The list of tenants, by now a long one, included Peugeot Cycles, Du Pont, Hawker Siddeley, International Computers, Yorkshire Imperial Metals and many other respected names including the Institution of Electrical Engineers. The efficiency of the Group's professional services was demonstrated by carrying out for Bishop's Stores a scheme for a 40,000 square feet Cash and Carry store. The parties first met on 16th February 1972 and the project was completed, ten days ahead of schedule, on 22nd August 1972. Many local authorities were well disposed towards the Group. The report mentions developments carried out in conjunction with nine such authorities and speaks of 'close co-operation with the Greater London Council Industrial Centre.'

Left to right:
Anthony Edmonds, Secretary of the Hunting Gate Group, with Christopher Sly and Jeremy Raisman, Partners of Jaques & Lewis, the Group's solicitors.

On the housing side, a considerable store of land had been built up and large new developments were planned near Luton, Bedford, Watford, Stevenage, Cambridge and Hitchin. The report exudes optimism: 'In anticipation that the house market in East Anglia will expand rapidly during the remainder of the '70's, a great increase of our activity in that area is expected in 1974/75 ... We will be offering a wider range of houses and flats than ever before, to ensure that there is something to interest every house purchaser.' All this would stretch the Group's resources much further than ever before. It was the particular speciality of the Joint Managing Director, David Moore.

If the Chairman felt any anxiety about the immediate future, or about the expansionist course on which the Group was set, he gave no public hint of it, except perhaps in a passing reference to 'the increasing cost of long term mortgages.' In 1972, even allowing for inflation, the figures showed that the business had done well, and he praised the work of the Architect's Department under Samuel Bettany* and John Washington; of the Legal Department under David Morgan; and of the Estates Department under Danny Desmond. He foresaw a turnover in house sales, during the year to come, considerably greater than £2 million; gross rental income of about £500,000; net profit 'well in excess of last year's figures.' If there was a storm coming, evidently the ill wind had not yet begun to blow.

* Since left

Warehouse and offices for Yorkshire Imperial Metals, Hitchin Industrial Estate. 1967.

A 40,000 sq.ft. Cash and Carry store for Bishops, Bedford. Completed in 1972, ten days ahead of schedule.

Chapter Six

STORM, STRESS AND RECOVERY

Storm, Stress and Recovery

During the seventies the long dream of everlasting, indestructible prosperity in which the nation's standard of living was carried almost effortlessly upward on a flowing tide of economic growth, began to fade. In its place a much bleaker reality emerged, especially after the Arabian oil producers suddenly realised how powerful they were, at the time of the Yom Kippur war in the Autumn of 1973, and began to advance the price of oil not by addition but by multiplication.

On all the industrial economies of the West the effect of the 'oil crisis' was serious. On the British economy it was devastating. Edward Heath's Government, after a promising start, came into collision with the trade unions, tried to enforce a 'pay policy', and was destroyed by the miners. The rate of inflation soared towards South American levels, reaching at one time 25 per cent a year. Unemployment, generally considered in the fifties and sixties to be a problem solved, began in the mid-seventies to climb.

In the turmoil of the times, the property market, which had flourished during the sixties under the influence of lively demand and relatively easy terms for borrowing money, took off into a boom, propelled along its upward path by an abundance of easy credit which accompanied Heath's policy of the 'Dash for Growth'. Nothing in property, it seemed in 1972-3, could go wrong. The price you paid today would be doubled when you sold tomorrow, and the day after that the next seller would get even more.

Prudence went overboard among lenders and borrowers alike. So great was the euphoria that some developers – not Frederick Bandet – began borrowing in order to pay interest on earlier loans. Moreover they borrowed short, for periods up to five years, for surely within that time they would sell again and take their profit or else they would get new finance for a longer term.

As is so often the case when a boom reaches a certain point, irrational optimism became infectious, just as irrational pessimism becomes infectious when the economic pendulum swings the other way. 'Developers' swarmed into the market, and, with a most unbankerly rashness, the banks – first of all the 'secondary' banks and foreign-owned banks, later the clearing banks and merchant banks – found them the finance they wanted without enquiring too closely whether they had the ability or the experience to put it to good use. So the merry dance went on, wilder still and wilder.

In the Autumn of 1973 property values reached their peak. By then the Arabs had realised the power of the 'oil weapon', inflation was frighteningly high, and the Government was going into reverse by making money very tight. Moreover, even to Conservatives the profits that were being made from trading in property were beginning to look like part of the 'unacceptable face of capitalism.' Anthony Barber, the Chancellor of the Exchequer, therefore imposed new and more stringent rules for the taxation of developers' profits, and brought them into his 'mini-budget' of December 1973.

Instead of paying Capital Gains Tax at 30% on the whole of any profit from disposals of industrial property (residential property was not affected), developers were henceforth required to pay corporation tax at 52% on the bulk of any profit over £1,000 if the profit amounted to more than one-fifth of the cost price or one-tenth of the current use value. Trading in industrial property was not at that time a conspicuous part of Frederick Bandet's business, and in themselves these rules might not have hurt him very much. What did hurt was an announcement by

Headlines in the National Press.

the Chancellor, at the same time as he brought them in, that when industrial property with a rent of more than £5,000 was let for the first time, the letting would be treated as a 'disposal' and profit arising from it would be taxed according to the new rules.

Payment could be spread over a period of years, but the immediate effect of the tax was to make the building of factories for lease – the central feature of Bandet's policy – a very unattractive proposition: the more so since, in a time of rapidly rising inflation, it was impossible to get the thirty-year mortgages at comparatively low rates of interest which had underpinned Bandet's business in the sixties. On top of everything else, a General Election early in 1974, brought about by the success of the coal miners' tactics in conducting their national strike, put a Labour Government into power and in May 1974 the Government froze commercial rents.

Property values collapsed, and the more speculative property enterprises collapsed with them. By May 1974 Harry Sonning's Guardian Properties, Ronnie Lyon's Ronald Lyon Holdings and William Stern's Wilstar Securities Group had all foundered, carrying with them assets valued at hundreds of millions of pounds. By the summer, property values generally had dropped, in a matter of months, by figures ranging between 25% and 50%.

The financial crisis which followed, in the Autumn of 1974, invites comparison with the greatest financial crises of the past: with the crisis which led to the devaluation of sterling in 1931; with the collapse of 1920 which was followed by a sudden rise in unemployment figures from 400,000 to 2,000,000; with the fall of Overend, Gurney in 1866; with the South Sea Bubble of 1720. The property disaster was not the sole cause but it was

The Midland Bank, Hitchin.

the proximate cause, transforming nervousness into panic and intensifying a fear, already present, that the social, political and economic framework of the national life was on the verge of dissolution. The stock market, as always a more reliable indicator of opinion than most opinion polls, crashed to its lowest levels since the early thirties. The banking system, from the secondary banks through to the more august institutions at its centre, seemed to be in grave danger, and the scale of rescue by the Bank of England's £1,300 million 'Lifeboat' was not measurable by that figure alone. Nevertheless, by means of the 'Lifeboat' and other measures, including large purchases of property by the 'institutions' (between 1975 and 1978 they put £4,392 million into property – more than twice as much as in the previous four years), the rescue worked. The sky remained suspended – just – and Earth's foundations stayed, but the 'glad confident morning' of the sixties had passed away for ever.

For Hunting Gate, nevertheless, the seventies began cheerfully enough, as Frederick Bandet's remarks in 1972 make clear. He went on bringing well-qualified professional men into the business, and in 1971 he engaged David Morgan, a 27-year-old solicitor educated at St. Catharine's College, Cambridge. He had served his articles with Coward Chance in London and then gained experience with them and with a local authority, which he found unexciting. For this reason an advertisement by Hunting Gate in the *Law Society Gazette* attracted him although he had no background in property – his family were in wholesale confectionery and tobacco – and at the time he joined the Group he knew no more of it than he could gather from a company search. He was interviewed by Frederick Bandet and David

The City of London.

Moore; they struck him, he says, as 'chalk and cheese.'

The Group's corporate structure, as we saw in Chapter Five, took the form of an alliance between operating companies and investment companies, linked to each other through Frederick Bandet, who controlled them all. In 1972, there were two operating companies, one in construction and one in housing, and nine investment companies.

'The intention', said Frederick Bandet in his statement, 'is to create a Group under the Hunting Gate name . . . this will be accompanied by the allotment of shares to the Directors in the construction and residential development companies. We hope that the Group will become progressively known as the Hunting Gate Group, whereas the Investment Companies which do not rely on publicity, will continue under their present names and generally as before.'

Frederick Bandet's financial objective in devising the structure of his business, as we observed in Chapter Four, was to build up the value of the property which the Investment Companies owned and not to make large profits from construction. The construction company therefore bought land, built factories – usually with short-term finance provided by the Midland Bank against guarantees from the other companies – and let them. When they were let they were sold to the Investment Companies. The selling price was crucial. It was settled at the cost of construction plus a percentage which until the mid-fifties was 10% and after that, 15%.

The essence of these arrangements, which was to become important later when the nature of the Group was under discussion, was that the various companies were regarded not as independent entities, but as parts of one organisation with one purpose in view: the maintenance and strengthening of the investment portfolio. Virtually all the assets were concentrated in the Investment Companies. The construction company had very little – scarcely a practical arrangement if the construction company had been intended to stand on its own. The true state of affairs was well understood at the Midland Bank and in Sun Life of Canada.

Mainly for the Bank and institutional lenders, 'combined accounts' were prepared from 1971 onward, designed to show the Group's expanding asset base and to demonstrate prudent management. They were not consolidated accounts prepared according to the rules of the Institute of Chartered Accountants because the companies were independent of each other in a formal sense, in spite of their close practical relationship. Nevertheless, they give a comprehensive view of the business, and those which accompany the Report and Accounts for 1972 show how it stood after eight or nine years of rapid expansion.

The 1972 combined balance sheets show the capital employed in the Group at just over £2 million, of which nearly £1.5 million was provided by long-term loans and mortgages and a further £768,125 by way of bank overdraft. It was represented by fixed assets of nearly £1.7 million, consisting chiefly of freehold and leasehold land. Current assets of £1.4 million included a stock of building land at £880,441. The freehold and leasehold land among the assets was shown at cost less depreciation whereas market value was likely to have been closer to £3.6 million; a point unlikely to be missed by institutions or by investment analysts.

The combined Profit and Loss Account for the Group showed net sales of just over £2 million, including nearly £1.9 million from sales of houses. Payments to sub-contractors (£788,064) the cost of land used (£327,535) and of materials (£354,585), as well as other relatively minor costs, brought the net income from house sales down to £454,188. Even so, it was greater than the gross income from rents–£346,534–from which outgoings, proportionately much lower, left a net income of £216,351. Finance costs (£167,315), Administration and Overheads (£165,394) and Directors' Salaries (£60,193) brought the Group profit before tax to £277,637.

What stands out from these figures is the rise in house sales, over about eight years, from nothing to almost £1.9 million. Measured in terms of income and profit, housing had become the Group's major activity, and it contributed handsomely to the flow of cash required to keep factory construction going.

With a prosperous business as large as Hunting Gate was becoming in the early seventies, the question of a public issue was sure to arise, and arise it did. Between 1971 and 1973, with the help of lawyers, accountants, merchant bankers and stockbrokers, the Directors of Hunting Gate explored the merits of the case. The more venturesome among them were no doubt attracted by the prospect of readier access to greater funds which the standing of a public company might open up. It would also make Hunting Gate shares marketable, which would hardly be unwelcome to Directors who were shareholders.

Frederick Bandet had his own position to consider. He had never found difficulty in financing any development which he considered prudent; did he need the wider access to funds which the standing of a public company might bring? Would it be worth sacrificing the privacy of a private company? Would it be worth any weakening, however slight, in his own control over his own creation, or any threat, however, distant, to the position of his family?

The events of 1973 – still more, the Stock Exchange collapse of 1974 – made his decision for him. He could not go to the market under those conditions. The question, however, remained: should he go to the market when he could?

The collapse of the property market in 1973 and the impact of the 'First Lettings Tax' came as a severe shock to Hunting Gate. It was the first serious setback the business had suffered, and it made nonsense of the high hopes of 1972. On the industrial side, even if demand for factories had been lively, rather than almost dead, the lettings tax would have made factory construction unattractive, and rents were frozen. On the housing side, mortgages became difficult and very expensive and Hunting Gate Homes found that the kind of houses they had been putting up were almost unsaleable. At one time they had sixty or seventy on their hands – all representing money on which interest had to be paid.

Frederick Bandet, unlike some of the more flamboyant developers, was not undone. His native caution and the solid assets of the Investment Companies prevented the Midland Bank from losing confidence in Hunting Gate and the business was never in danger. Nevertheless, for two or three years after 1973 there was no expansion; only a grim struggle to hold on. Office staff were reduced to a level which the rental income could carry. Building land not immediately required was sold, bringing in about £1 million. Income was not used to finance new development but to service reduced borrowings. Not once did the Company need to discuss its commitments with the Bank, nor was interest ever 'rolled over'.

In 1970 or thereabouts, the rate at which the business was growing caused David Moore to survey his own prospects. He had been with Hunting Gate, by then, about six years, and he told both Frederick Bandet and Keith Guyton that if he were to remain as Managing Director he would want a change in his conditions of service, and the change would not be small. Whereas in the past he had shared in the growth of the business to the extent of 10%, he now considered, in his own words, that 'an appropriate and proper figure' would be 30%.

At intervals over a year or so this bold proposal was discussed, but no attempt was made to get an independent assessment of it. At first no bitterness was evident – that came later – but Frederick Bandet was deeply disturbed. He had often told Moore that he didn't want a partner, and now he felt that Moore 'wanted to take over effective control of my Group': an ambition which he would never under any circumstances countenance. To such a situation there could only be one outcome. In 1974 David Moore left Hunting Gate, very handsomely compensated indeed.

'I've always tried', says Frederick Bandet, 'to recruit two opposing elements.' One he defines as "the go-getters", the business getters. The other he identifies with accountants, 'who keep a strict eye on the desirability, the feasibility of the proposal before we go into it.' Business getters, he says, are usually extroverts. 'They have to have tremendous staying power – physical power and emotional stamina – because the rejections, the things that don't come off, far outweigh the successes . . . You need people . . . who have ambition, physical stamina, and drive, who work long hours and come up with opportunities

. . . they like fast cars . . . some smoke cigars.'

'These people', he says, no doubt with truth, 'are not your average accountants.'

Moore had been a business getter. So is Danny Desmond. After Moore left, Desmond became Deputy Managing Director, an appointment which proclaimed the crucial importance to the Group of the kind of ability, not easily defined in professional terms, which Desmond so conspicuously displays.

In January 1974, following his principle of balance, Frederick Bandet made a very different appointment. After a long search for the right man, he engaged a taciturn Scottish Chartered Accountant, W.D. Deans, as Financial Controller. Later, he was appointed to the Group Board as Financial Director. Deans brought with him professional skill developed in the service of John Laing Properties and Brixton Estates Limited. His skill was of a kind not previously applied to Hunting Gate's affairs, but in the opinion of some competent observers, it was needed.

Deans's immediate advice to Frederick Bandet was to turn the wretched state of the property market to his advantage by a process which he called 'taking a bath'. The value of land holdings had fallen, so Deans's suggestion was that Hunting Gate's land holdings should be substantially written down. The suggestion was accepted, and the result in 1974 was a 'book' loss – the only loss in the Group's history – of £262,000. In later years, as business improved, profits were shown on the reduced values and industrial building allowances were set off against them, which had been part of Deans's intention.

Deans was important to Bandet, and Bandet to Deans. Deans performed the function Bandet required – to hold the balance between the energies of the 'business-getter' and the more prosaic demands of a sound commercial enterprise. Bandet presented Deans with an opportunity to do what he was good at – and in the process to make money – on a scale Deans could hardly have dreamed possible when he was first interviewed. Bandet quickly came to appreciate the value of an alert professional mind, and equally quickly – in contrast to his usual caution in such matters – he came to place great confidence in Deans.

As these changes were taking place in Hunting Gate's management – the departure of Moore, the promotion of Desmond, the appointment of Deans – economic conditions in Great Britain were forcing changes in the way the Hunting Gate business would in future be run. On the industrial side, high rates of inflation, rising rapidly, not only destroyed long-term fixed-interest mortgages but at the same time brought more and more money into the hands of financial institutions, particularly pension funds, who had to find uses for it. Property attracted them, as it had done for some time, but they were not equipped, nor did they wish to equip themselves, for the whole process of property development. They needed the expertise of property developers to give them opportunities to buy newly built factories, offices and shops, in desirable localities, which had already been let to first-class tenants. On the housing side, demand for the three- and four-bedroom houses which Hunting Gate had been accustomed to build remained weak, but there was an unsatisfied demand for houses within the means of people buying for the first time – houses with two bedrooms, or perhaps only one, and the minimum of expensive fittings.

Thus, although building for sale to the Investment Companies would remain important, it became apparent that building for sale outside the Group altogether, both on the industrial and the housing sides, was likely to assume an importance in the future much greater than in the past. The skills required in the Group – skills of acquisition, designing, building, letting – would be the same, but instead of being used almost entirely for the service of the Investment Companies they would be used in the same way for the benefit of pension funds, insurance companies – and first-time buyers.

Chapter Seven

CALIFORNIA!

California!

As the nature of Hunting Gate's business in the United Kingdom began to change, possibilities further afield were coming over the horizon. At first the obvious direction to look seemed to be towards the Continent, for in the sixties and early seventies there was a vogue among British business men, property developers included, for "going into Europe." Continental economies seemed to offer much greater opportunities for expansion than the economy at home: it seemed sensible to take advantage of them.

The difficulties turned out to be formidable; difficulties not only of language but of law and administration; of business usage (corruption, in some countries, not excluded); and of culture generally. Moreover, some British business men assumed, quite without justification, that their methods, particularly perhaps in marketing, were far ahead of anything known to the rather primitive continentals, especially in the Latin countries. For a variety of reasons several British businesses, among them ICI, Metal Box and Bowater, had unfortunate adventures beyond the Channel.

In 1972 Frederick Bandet, continental himself in origin, went to a conference arranged in Paris for British property developers. He went to look at the possibilities open to Hunting Gate and decided against them. 'As far as my English team were concerned', he says, 'the various languages and differing administrative procedures and systems put the European Continent further away than Canada or the USA.'

He went further. With his continental background he was able to take a far more detached view of the North Atlantic countries than any native of them was likely to be capable of, and to him the similarities loomed much larger than the differences. 'In my own perception', he says, 'in my own feelings,

Britain, the US and Canada have always formed one single entity, despite all I know to the contrary. I got used to moving about freely in this entity a long time before contemplating the move to California. For long my vision, and my intention, was to spread the assets of the Group (and therefore my own) throughout this entity together with the activities of the Group and of my family.'

To spread assets is also to spread risks, and Frederick Bandet in 1974-5 felt strongly that they should be spread. In the depressed state of the British economy, the most he could look for in his own business was stability, and that only by avoiding undue risk with even greater determination than usual. Stability is not far removed from stagnation, and stagnation in the United Kingdom seemed to Frederick Bandet the signal for expansion elsewhere. For him, 'elsewhere' could hardly be anywhere except North America.

He was not alone among British property developers in looking across the Atlantic. As early as 1973 the Pan Am building, supported above Grand Central Station on a foundation of British capital, was known in New York as 'Great Britain's revenge for the London Hilton'. Since then many firms in the property business, including Richard Ellis, a London firm of chartered surveyors with whom Hunting Gate has had many dealings, have been very busy in the United States.

Perhaps there was a deeper reason for Frederick Bandet's restlessness. His political nose is very sensitive. In the late thirties he had smelt danger in Czecho-Slovakia long before most people would take the idea seriously. Did he in the mid-seventies sniff danger in what was superficially the most unlikely place of all: Great Britain? Political conditions were very disturbed and violence, during the miners' strike of 1973-4,

San Francisco Bay Area showing developments as at July 1983.

San Francisco.

was never far away. If Heath had won the first election of 1974, there might have been bloodshed. Even the unthinkable – a military *coup* – came briefly within the range of thought. Having seen his family overwhelmed by political disaster once, Bandet could hardly be blamed if he took care to see that his family would not be overwhelmed again.

One thing is certain. In contemplating the United States for his business, Bandet was not seeking a 'tax haven' for himself. If he had been looking for a 'tax haven', he would not have chosen the USA. Tax rates may be rather lower than in the United Kingdom, but a United States resident with investments abroad must face very rigorous scrutiny from the Internal Revenue Service, which seems to work on the assumption that capital invested outside the United States must be invested for some nefarious purpose. If lower taxation had been Bandet's principal aim, he would probably have gone to Switzerland, a country he knows well and is fond of, where his mother tongue is spoken.

As Bandet began to take the idea of American expansion seriously, it became clear to him that there would be far-reaching consequences for himself and his family as well as for his business. He had seen property developers come to grief in Europe trying to act as absentee investors, and he had no mind to make the same mistake himself in America. He did not at first contemplate permanent emigration, but he did intend to spend a good deal of his time there, during all or part of which his family would be with him.

'Time spent on reconnaissance', they say in the army, 'is never wasted'. Bandet and Desmond made wide reconnaissances in North America. They went to Canada. They looked at the Eastern seaboard of the United States. They spent a good deal of time in Philadelphia, where they examined investment projects and made useful contacts. Then Desmond moved three thousand miles Westward, to San Francisco, to investigate and make recommendations. His professional knowledge, set off by his friendly personality, brought him valuable contacts, and his assessment of possibilities encouraged Bandet, in the middle of 1975, to go and see it for himself. He was impressed.

Northern California, Bandet decided, was the place for his new venture, roughly within a 35 – 45 mile radius of San Francisco. That area includes 'Silicon Valley', stretching southward toward San José, where the revolution in information science was born which promises to bring about social and economic changes as great, perhaps, as those precipitated by the development of steam power. High technology flourishes there, not so much in production as in research and development, and it has been far less seriously affected by recession than areas such as Detroit, where older forms of manufacturing industry predominate. In fact, Silicon Valley hardly knows what recession means. It is still a place for young men with bright ideas, and the ideas still come thick and fast, so that what is the newest thing today is obsolete in two years' time. It is very much the sort of area where a developer interested in factories, offices and shops might prosper.

Besides Silicon Valley, the area round San Francisco Bay includes San Francisco itself, its prosperous suburbs, and two world-class universities: Berkeley and Stanford. Its benign climate makes it a most agreeable place to live – a point taken by Frederick Bandet – which makes it easy to attract scientists and technologists who are paid well enough to afford extravagant house prices, though by the same token it makes ordinary factory labour almost impossible to obtain.

All in all, perhaps no part of the Western industrial world shines so brightly as Northern California through the economic gloom of the late seventies and early eighties. So, at any rate, thought Frederick Bandet in 1975, and he flew his family over there – the first time any of them had flown: Bandet does not take risks lightly – to test their reactions. They drove from Los Angeles to San Francisco, then flew across the continent for a holiday in Maine, driving from Boston to Keyzar Lake on the Canadian border. They saw no reason to quarrel with Bandet's preference for California as a place to live.

As soon as Frederick Bandet had decided to go to California, the question of a visa arose. He and his advisers intended applying for a visa which was available under the classification 'Inter-Company Transferee' which would allow him to spend three to five years in the United States without further formalities until it came up for renewal. A fresh application would then have to be made, with the remote but real possibility that renewal might be refused. With the help of Jeremy Raisman a proposal was drafted and Bandet took it to the American Consul in London as the official responsible for granting visas.

The Consul realised that Bandet had substantial funds for investment in America. On that basis he would be welcome not merely as a visitor but as a permanent resident. Permanent residence in America is not lightly offered to foreigners, but the consul offered it to Bandet. 'You know, Mr. Bandet,' he said, 'you'd be far better off with full immigration visas for yourself and your family.' Bandet, naturally, was flattered. Moreover, he fully appreciated the advantages of not having to go through the renewal process for the temporary visa. He felt at ease in America and had no qualms about living there. Perhaps he did not go as fully into the implications of an immigrant's visa as he

might have done; a curious and uncharacteristic omission. Strongly encouraged by some of his colleagues, and against the advice of others, he accepted the American Consul's offer.

Arranging Bandet's affairs so that he could take up permanent residence in the United States with the least unpleasant tax consequences was a complicated process. His legal and financial advisers, amongst whom Deans was prominent, carried it through with great efficiency, but when matters had gone so far as to be virtually unstoppable, certain requirements began to emerge which, if Bandet had known of them from the first, might have given him pause.

He was disconcerted to find that, in order to establish beyond doubt his firm intention to leave Great Britain and settle in California, it would be advisable for him to sell both his flats in Campden Hill Gate and his house at Gosmore. That house meant a great deal to him. It symbolised both his success and his links with Hitchin, where his success had its foundations. He did not like getting rid of it, but the need was paramount.

On the business side, at an advanced stage in the proceedings, and for the same reason as that given for selling his flats and his house, Frederick Bandet's advisers urged the necessity of a very drastic step indeed. They told him that he should resign all his directorships in the Hunting Gate Group and the Investment Companies. He had no intention of retiring, and this forced separation from the business which he had created was deeply wounding. Moreover, there would be important practical consequences. In managing the Group's affairs the

Previous spread: 633 Menlo Avenue, Menlo Park, California, built to house Hunting Gate Management Company Inc. 1980.

Directors could with perfect legality carry most matters to completion and others a very long way without consulting Bandet. Bandet had to divest himself of all executive authority, leaving himself with nothing but his prestige as the founder and his large shareholdings in the capital of the Group and of the Investment Companies.

In 1980, as a further step in Americanising Bandet's affairs, it became desirable to 'expatriate' his family trusts, bringing them under American law and requiring a change of trustees. Under the new dispensation, the first-named trustee was Hans Frank, an elderly lawyer of great distinction who, like Bandet, had been born in Europe. He was the senior partner of Fried, Frank, Harris, Shriver & Jacobson, among the ten largest firms of attorneys in New York. He could be relied upon, in the conduct of his duties, to take an independent line.

Having taken advice, Frederick Bandet accepted it. On 19th March 1976 he resigned from the Board of Hunting Gate Limited and from the Board of the Investment Companies. On 27th July he arrived in California.

In California, Frederick Bandet intended to follow principles which had served him well in England. Slowly and carefully, one step at a time, relying chiefly on his own resources, he would build up, for the benefit of himself and his family, a portfolio of property investments. Finance would come largely from the rapidly increasing income of the Investment Companies; possibly from American partners. For technical services, if he could not find them locally, he would call on Hunting Gate in England.

In this deliberate way he approached the setting-up of an American headquarters in Menlo Park, one of the string of small and smallish towns which stretches away for thirty or forty miles on the peninsula south-eastward of San Francisco towards Silicon Valley. He chose a site in a street next to Santa Cruz Avenue, the most important shopping street where all the banks are. The price, he thought, was high, but he had no hesitation in paying it.

A couple of miles from Menlo Park lies Atherton, solely a residential community. It has a city hall, but no shops or commercial premises. The people who live there are generally very well-to-do – each house must be detached on at least an acre – and they like a short journey to their offices. Frederick Bandet lives in Atherton.

To buy a site for his office was one thing; to build on it, quite another. He turned to local firms for plans and estimates, establishing himself meanwhile in rented accommodation. Plans took a long time to prepare, estimates turned out too high, and it was a matter of years before he found a firm to do what he wanted at a price he would pay.

Then he sent for Eric Howlett, who – as is his way – made things happen, partly by force of personality, partly, where necessary, by physical demonstration of the skills of the building trade. In 1980, the building at 633 Menlo Avenue was ready, providing about 8,000 sq. feet of space on two floors. About four years after he moved to California, Frederick Bandet and his assistant Helen Ergil sat down for the first time in Bandet's own American office.

The organisation of the business in California follows the same general principles as those underlying the organisation in England. Soon after he came to America in 1976, Bandet set up an American company, Hunting Gate Management Company Inc., to manage the investments he was planning to

Frederick Bandet in his office at Menlo Park with Helen Ergil, his Executive Assistant.

make. This is the company which has its offices in Menlo Park. There is also Erecta Properties (North America), incorporated in the state of Delaware with a capital of $1 million for the purpose of trading in property. Parallel with the American companies, but with offices in San Francisco, Hunting Gate Group in 1980 established a subsidiary of its own, Hunting

A meeting of Hunting Gate Management Company Inc. in the Board Room at Menlo Park, California.
Left to right: Marcia McChrystal, Stanley Thomas, Frederick Bandet, Henry Bandet, Jeffie Feakins.

Gate Pacific Limited. It is an English company and it stands in the same relationship to Hunting Gate Management as Hunting Gate Group in England stands to the Investment Companies there; separate but related.

In 1979 Frederick Bandet engaged David Harrison, an undergraduate at Stanford University two or three miles along the road from Menlo Park, to drive his car during the university vacation. Harrison, born 3,000 miles away in Pennsylvania, had decided that Stanford was the university for him, and he had been aiming at an MBA after graduation.

Bandet took to the young man (he was born in 1958) as in the past he had taken to other young men of evident talent but without experience, and offered him a permanent job. Harrison, on the bird-in-hand principle, accepted, working at first as deputy to Howlett on the Menlo Avenue building site. By 1982, with two or three years' general training in the property business behind him, he felt he had outgrown anything Hunting Gate Management could at that time offer him. Bandet passed him on to Hunting Gate Pacific in San Francisco. Once again, having spotted a young man with talent, he opened the way for him to develop it.

Underlying the other managerial appointments which have so far been made in California, it may be possible to detect another of Frederick Bandet's guiding principles: holding the balance between the 'business-getter' and the accountant. In an office in Montgomery Street in the heart of San Francisco's financial district, Ian B. Paget ARICS presides with breezy confidence over the business of Hunting Gate Pacific. He was born in 1949 and learned the property business during nine years with Keith Cardale Groves, one of London's larger firms of chartered surveyors. Before he came to Hunting Gate, he

Ian Paget and David Harrison explaining a prospective development to Gina Bandet (second from right) at Hunting Gate Pacific's offices in Montgomery Street, San Francisco. Debra Cloud, secretary to Ian Paget, looks on.

Office building at San Rafael, California. Completed 1980.

Research and development building in Silicon Valley at 2660 Marine Way, Mountain View, California. Completed 1980.

A retail development at Mill Valley, California, completed 1983.

had two years as Vice-President of Keith Cardale Groves in Beverley Hills. He looks very much like a permanent British export to the USA.

Stanley E. Thomas, Vice-President of Hunting Gate Management Company, served as a naval officer in Vietnam, then took an MBA at Stanford – the degree David Harrison had been aiming at – and then qualified as a Certified Public Accountant while working with Deloitte Haskins & Sells in San Francisco. Later on he had six years of managerial experience, chiefly in the field of taxation, with rapidly growing high technology firms in Silicon Valley. The property business is new to him, but Thomas's quiet financial professionalism is as important to it as Paget's entrepreneurial energy.

It cannot yet be said that Frederick Bandet has done more in California than lay the foundations of future growth. Half a dozen projects, including office, factory and shop property, have been undertaken and more are being considered, but the scale of operations is tiny in comparison with those in the United Kingdom.

This is in character. Frederick Bandet did not look for rapid growth during his early years in the United Kingdom and he has said that growth in California is bound for some time to be slow. How rapid it may be, once the foundations have been soundly laid, will be apparent when we consider Hunting Gate's progress in the United Kingdom during the years when the Californian business was being set up; that is, from 1976 to 1982.

Chapter Eight

THE GREAT EXPANSION 1976-81

The Great Expansion 1976 - 81

IN the history of nearly every successful business there comes a moment when the founder must hand over control, willingly or otherwise, to his successors. In many businesses it is a moment of crisis. It can never be without risk. For Hunting Gate it arrived, unexpectedly, when Frederick Bandet, acting on advice tendered for reasons which had nothing to do with his competence as a manager or a business man, reluctantly resigned executive office in the enterprise which he had brought into existence.

When Bandet gave up the Chairmanship, it ceased to be an executive post and passed to Keith Guyton. There was one other non-executive Director: Michael Barnes. Executive authority passed to the four men whom Bandet had selected for it over the years: Danny Desmond as Managing Director, Bill Deans as Deputy Managing Director, Eric Howlett as Construction Director and David Morgan, Group Solicitor co-opted to the Board. Since then, Morgan has taken responsibility for the Group's Public Relations and Advertising; he has led the Group's sponsorship of sport (he is Chairman of Hitchin Town Football Club); and he has played a major role in the development of the housing company.

The capital structure of the business which the Directors were to run was re-constructed, partly by increasing the authorised share capital from £1,000 to £50,000, all of which was immediately issued, partly by converting advances from the Investment Companies into an unsecured nine-year loan of £550,000 at a fixed rate of interest – 12% – very favourable to Hunting Gate. Overdraft facilities from the Midland Bank, a central pillar of Bandet's financial planning, continued as before and, as before, without any massive asset backing in the balance sheet of Hunting Gate Group, which for 1975-6 showed fixed assets of £60,840 and net current assets of £724;554, financed by shareholders' funds of £90,394, deferred taxation of £145,000, and the unsecured loan of £550,000. A bank overdraft of £377,384 appears among the current liabilities.

Figures like these, which were all that were shown in the published accounts of the Hunting Gate Group, prompted uncharitable critics to the accusation that Bandet had decamped 6,000 miles leaving to his successors a company with little in the way of assets and a mountain of debt. What these critics overlooked, because the figures did not appear in the Group's accounts, were the assets of the Investment Companies amounting to about £9 million, which were fundamental to the financial soundness of the Group although the Investment Companies formed no part of it, nor was the overdraft secured on them. The Midland Bank, nevertheless, knew Frederick Bandet. In the days of crisis, not long past,he had never sought to re-arrange loans, never asked the Bank to 'roll-up' interest, had always met his obligations in full. If a company in which Bandet had a large interest wanted a loan, the Listening Bank would not be deaf.

Besides the 'invisible' and apparently unmentionable comfort which the Investment Companies provided for the Hunting Gate Group, they also provided a secure source of income, for the Group undertook, for a fee, the management of the Investment Companies' properties, and the fee was set, to start with, at 12½% of the gross rents. Rental income stood at £934,000 in 1976, and in four years it rose to £1,867,000. When a consultancy agreement with Bandet, set up in 1976, was terminated, in 1981, the fee charge to the Investment Companies was brought down, ultimately, to 7% of the rental income, but even at that figure it provided a secure and rapidly rising element in the Group's total income: a welcome insurance, especially in the early days,

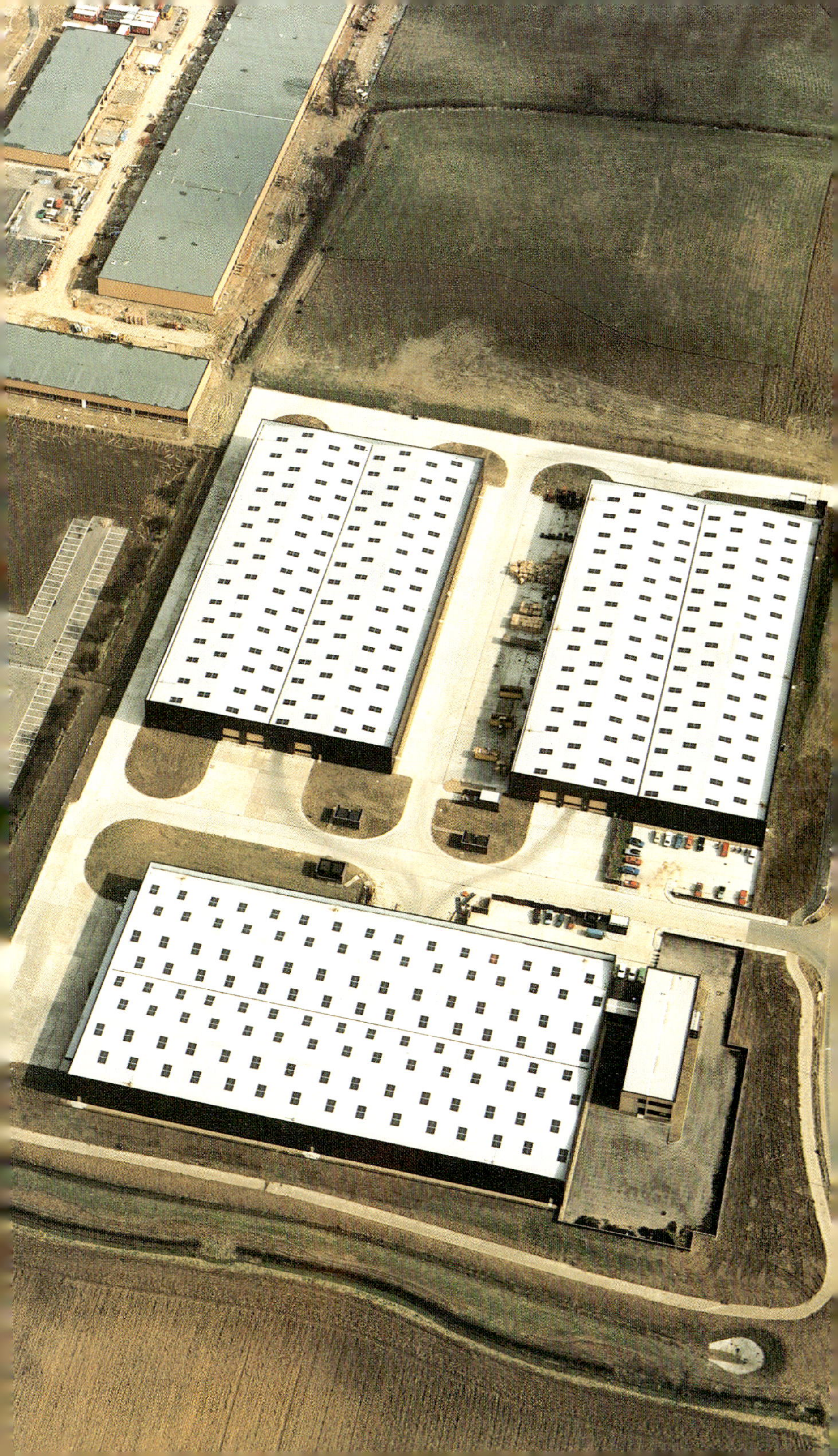

against the inevitable risks of property development.

One other advantage the management of the Investment Companies' property also conferred on Hunting Gate Group. The Group became very well acquainted with the Investment Companies' tenants, and from time to time a tenant might become a customer for factories or other buildings put up by the Group's construction company, as Schuberts did when they moved from a building rented from one of the Investment Companies at Hitchin into a 250,000 sq. ft. factory built for them – by Hunting Gate – at Peterborough.

In dealing with the Investment Companies, the Group was in much the same position as a merchant bank dealing with investment clients. The Group had a duty to see that attractive opportunities were offered to the Companies. If they were not taken up, then the Group could take them up itself or offer them elsewhere.

The Investment Companies, therefore, were in more than one way a source of strength to the Hunting Gate Group. To Frederick Bandet, they were the pivot on which the whole system turned. Whatever other activities the Board of Hunting Gate might go in for, it remained their paramount duty, in Bandet's opinion, to see to the interest of the Investment Companies, which were overwhelmingly the interests of himself and his family. Whatever the legal form might be of the business which Frederick Bandet had founded, the Group and the Investment Companies, to his way of thinking, were parts of an indivisible whole. The agreement under which the Group managed them, nevertheless, was an informal one which had come into existence

Previous page: A 250,000 sq. ft. industrial development for Panel Plus Industries at Orton Southgate, Peterborough, 1981.

while the whole business was under Bandet's personal control. It had never been put into writing. There would have been no point in doing so, for it would have been as if F. Bandet was making an agreement with Bandet F.

Before Bandet left, he offered shares in Hunting Gate Group, to be supplied from his personal holding, to the four executive directors, who were invited to buy them on very favourable terms. His offer was taken up, and the result was that Bandet's personal holding in the Group fell from 49½% to 34½% and the holdings of the directors rose from 25% to 37½%. The total Bandet holdings, directly and through the trusts, dropped from 77½% to 62½%. The move was a generous one. Some of its results were unforeseen.

However the matter is looked at, it is clear that Frederick Bandet's resignation presented the executive directors, perhaps more than half involuntarily, with such an opportunity as comes to few business men. They succeeded to the control of an organisation which had built and sold well over a hundred factories and a much greater number of houses; which had plenty of profitable work in progress, satisfactorily financed; which had a staff, sixty or seventy strong by 1976, technically and professionally qualified to carry on and expand the Group's activities. The penalty of enterprise is risk, but the risk to themselves as individuals was not great, since their salaries and overheads were amply covered by the management fees from the Investment Companies, and they were not required to give personal financial guarantees. They could concentrate with an easy mind on building up the business.

They were a strong and well balanced team, chosen for the positions they held by Bandet himself. One of the two Managing Directors – Desmond – was a first class property developer and business getter; the other – Deans – a skilful, strong minded financial planner. Desmond, though recruited and trained by Bandet, and full of respect for him, was not at all of Bandet's cautious temperament, and when Bandet went abroad there is no doubt that Desmond felt the brakes had been taken off. Bandet, still by far the largest individual shareholder, could and did keep in touch with the business on which all his hopes and plans rested, and in which he had so much emotional capital invested, by assiduous reading of papers, by daily telephone calls, by occasional visits, but he no longer held executive office. He was usually six thousand miles away, and he was dealing with men of strong character and proven ability, with views of their own on how Hunting Gate should be run. Moreover, he had admitted them to participation in the ownership of Hunting Gate but not in the ownership of the Investment Companies, and they might not feel quite the same regard for the importance of the Investment Companies as he did.

Hunting Gate Group Limited, of which Desmond, Deans, Howlett and Morgan were Directors, was – and is – a holding company which in 1976 had six subsidiaries. Two – Hunting Gate Construction Limited and Hunting Gate Homes Limited – were operating companies. Of the rest, three were investment companies holding property on behalf of the Group rather than Bandet, and one was Hunting Gate Design Consultants Limited. Hunting Gate Developments Limited, so important today, had not yet been set up.

This was the organisation placed at the executive directors' disposal. To get a fair idea of the use they made of it during the late seventies it is desirable to look at figures for the Group and Bandet's Investment Companies taken together. Looked at in this way, the combined assets, £9.4 million in 1976, were 3 times greater (£29.8 million) in 1982, but the turnover in 1982–£34.6

6,600 sq.ft. office development for Welsmere Building Management Limited (a subsidiary of Debenhams Limited) at Basingstoke, 1981.

million–was 11½ times greater than the turnover (£3 million) four years earlier. Between 1976 and 1982 the net surplus before tax also went up about 9½ times, from £0.3 million to nearly 2.8 million.

These figures make no allowance for inflation, which was running high. The figures of turnover and surplus, however, must surely represent considerable growth. The number of people employed in the business increased during the late seventies as the various service departments were built up to cope with extra work coming into them. By 1979, the staff had more than doubled to 180, and by 1983 had increased again to 248.

If this is a picture of a business growing rapidly, it is also a picture of a business changing rapidly. More and more, the economic tide has carried the Group into building commercial properties for sale to financial institutions or, by way of 'design-and-build' services (largely the creation of Eric Howlett and his team), for sale to those who intend to occupy them, rather than for sale to the Investment Companies, and house-building for sale to owner-occupiers – the responsibility particularly of David Morgan – has increased in importance. The scale and geographical spread of Hunting Gate's operations, as they developed after 1976, are best appreciated from illustrations, but it may be observed that some are very large, such as the 123,000 sq. ft. of offices, factory and social facilities for BOC at Ramsgate in Kent or the 250,000 sq. ft. factory for Schuberts at Peterborough, and that the list of clients and tenants carries some most impressive names.

Force of circumstances no doubt dictated change in the general direction of Hunting Gate's policy, but it was a change highly congenial to the 'business-getter's' mentality; less so, perhaps, to Frederick Bandet's own. It was certainly far more noticeable than the way he had conducted the business in the past, and it was duly noticed. Press comment appeared which seemed to him to imply that the real growth of Hunting Gate had only begun after the founder had left, and at much the same time he began to worry about the well-being of the Investment Companies. He became deeply disturbed.

His anxieties were brought to a head by a renewed proposal for a public issue. It had been written into the Group's corporate plan in 1976, and in 1979 Bandet made it clear that he 'was prepared to accept the aim of a flotation . . . provided that such an acceptance is not taken as a commitment on his part. He also said that such an acceptance was subject to arrangements being made so that in the event of a flotation the control of the Group by himself and the Trust jointly would not be impaired.'

Those who urged the proposal argued, broadly, that the status of a public company would give Hunting Gate greater prestige in general and, in particular, easier access to funds, and that shares with an established market value could be used to acquire other companies. It would also put a precise value on the holdings of the Directors and they would no longer be so firmly locked into Hunting Gate.

Against that, it could be urged that the standing of Hunting Gate as a private company was perfectly adequate for all its requirements, and that the Group could raise all the funds it needed without going to the trouble and expense – very considerable – of a public issue. Moreover, although in some ways the Directors might gain from 'going public', they stood to lose a good deal from giving up the privacy of a private company.

Notwithstanding the fairly even balance of advantage on each side of the question, the matter was carried briskly forward during the first seven or eight months of 1981, apparently without

Captain Mark Phillips taking the Double Trouble fence at Brigstock Horse Trials in 1982, one of the several sporting events sponsored by Hunting Gate.

Hitchin Town Football Club, sponsored by Hunting Gate.

keeping Bandet fully informed or paying much attention to his special interests. He does not seem to have discovered quite how far matters had gone, and quite how his interests were likely to be affected, until July or August. Then he disconcerted the supporters of the proposition by abruptly announcing his total opposition. They could not proceed, because he held enough votes to block the indispensable alteration to the Articles of Association.

His interests were distinct from those of the executive directors. The terms of an issue could and no doubt would have been made most attractive to him on a short and narrow view, and perhaps for his lifetime, but in the long run Hunting Gate as a public company would almost certainly have slipped away from the control of the Bandet family, especially if their holding had been gradually diluted by share exchanges. This was not a prospect which Bandet was prepared to entertain, nor did he care for the possibility that the livelihood of Hunting Gate employees might at some time in the future be threatened by policies which he could not influence.

His dislike of the proposal was brought sharply into focus by the matter of the Investment Companies. If Hunting Gate went public, the Investment Companies' properties could no longer be managed in the old informal way. There would have to be a written agreement, and that agreement would provide for the possibility of withdrawal by either side. If at some time – perhaps no very distant time – in the future the Board of Hunting Gate wished to cut their connection with the Investment Companies, they could do so, and the essential unity of Frederick Bandet's business, on which he sets such store, would be shattered. Nothing in the world would make him risk that possibility–certainly not the questionable advantages of a public issue.

March 1982, Wyndham Thomas, Director General of the Peterborough Development Corporation, opens the 250,000 sq. ft. factory and warehousing development for Panel Plus Industries at Orton Southgate, Peterborough. Mr. Thomas is talking to Frederick Bandet and his daughter, Isabel.

Offices and factory for Fluke International Corporation at Watford, 1978.

This lamentable episode stirred up great rancour, particularly between Bandet and Deans. It reflects little credit on any of the parties. The Board should no doubt have paid greater attention to the interests of the largest shareholder, and they should have made sure of his support at every stage. The largest shareholder, on the other hand, should surely have been less equivocal in his attitude to the proposal and should have made his views known much earlier. The transatlantic telephone, it appears, is no adequate substitute for face-to-face communication.

What emerged very clearly from the turmoil was the need for strong representation of Bandet's interests on the Hunting Gate Board, and Bandet arranged for J.R. Cowen, then aged 49, to become a non-executive Director. He was appointed on 23rd September 1981. He had held high positions with De La Rue and Norcros. He had been Chief Executive of Henry Ansbacher & Co., merchant bankers, and he had gained knowledge of the Construction and Property Industry as Chairman of Dow-Mac Concrete Limited, and of Temperature Limited, manufacturers of air-conditioning and heating equipment. He had experience of Board Room practice and procedure and a shrewd understanding of corporate politics. Three months after his appointment, having conceived considerable respect for Bandet, he agreed to represent him and his family, full-time, in all Bandet's business interests in the United Kingdom, making the description 'non-executive' somewhat misleading.

As Cowen joined the Board, the King over the Water came into his own again. On 23rd September 1981 Frederick Bandet, no longer obliged to demonstrate the reality of his move to America, rejoined the Board of Hunting Gate Group as a non-executive Director and accepted election as President.

Deans, handsomely compensated, resigned from Hunting Gate

Offices and Banking Hall for Midland Bank, High Street, Crawley 1981.

One and two-bedroom flats over 25,000 sq. ft. retail store at Poynters Road, Luton, 1981.

75,000 sq. ft. of warehousing for Bosch at Watford, 1978.

65,000 sq. ft. of offices and warehousing for the Goodyear Tyre & Rubber Company, at Borehamwood 1977.

Supermarket for J. Sainsbury, at Mitcham, 1980.

on the last day of 1981. His place was filled, during 1982, by Nigel Turnbull, a forty-year-old Scottish Chartered Accountant with the degree of LLB from Edinburgh, who had made his career in finance and merchant banking, having held positions with Hill Samuel, Ansbacher, Lloyds and Scottish, and with Noble Grossart. The Hunting Gate Group had turned a corner: the most dangerous corner in its history so far.

Chapter Nine

'F B'

'FB'

THIS book, in the end, is not about a business but about a personality: the personality of "FB"; of Frederick Bandet. After looking at what he has built, what can we say about the builder?

The Nazi assault on Central Europe in the nineteen-thirties has dictated the pattern of Frederick Bandet's life. Because of it, he left Czecho-Slovakia, and persuaded his parents that they ought to leave, in 1939. Because of it, he suffered the worst personal injury of his life: the loss of his parents, and that still plunges him from time to time into agonies of self-accusation, though the real fault lay with the Home Office.

Then again, what has he been doing, these last forty years and more, if not seeking the security which he knew as a child, and which the Nazis destroyed? That security rested within the interlinked framework of a stable family and a well run family business; a framework which he has sought to re-create in England and in California.

The importance which Frederick Bandet attaches to the well-being of his family has been an unbroken thread in the pattern of effort which for so many years he has devoted to building up his business. It has run through all his closest personal relationships, especially the great affection which he feels for his children. It is this more than anything which gives landed property – 'real estate'–its immense attraction for him: an attraction at least as great as that felt by members of any great family – Russells, Cavendishes, Cecils, whom you will – towards their ancestral acres. It is this which gives the investment companies their place in his scheme of things and which causes him to react so fiercely if he thinks they are under threat or unfairly neglected.

The Hunting Gate business, besides being a guarantee of Frederick Bandet's security, is also an extension of his family.

He is fiercely possessive of it, and towards the people who work in it he feels responsibility, affection and loyalty. If he thinks that work has been well done, he says so, and his unobtrusive generosity, over the years, has been extensive. In return, loyalty is what he expects from his employees and he is deeply hurt if he does not find it. If the word 'paternalism' did not, today, carry unfortunate implications, then Bandet would be well described as a paternalistic employer.

It is consistent with Frederick Bandet's preoccupation with security that the characteristic above all others which everyone who deals with him remarks upon, and indeed which he remarks upon himself, is caution, even pessimism, leading to an insistence on looking at the worst possible outcome of any proposition, and a reluctance to commit himself to a decision with any serious element of risk in it. These are not qualities which one would expect in a property developer, and those in whom the property developer's instinct – the instinct of an optimistic risk-taker – is highly developed sometimes find them frustrating. They are not, however, negative qualities, for they have served Bandet well in building Hunting Gate on a more solid foundation than that of more showy enterprises. Moreover, the discipline which they impose on ebullience, as at least one 'business-getter' admits with gratitude, is salutary.

The picture of Frederick Bandet which emerges from a study of his career is not, then, the conventional picture of a property developer, nor of the *entrepreneur* of free enterprise folklore. He shows no eagerness to take risks or make decisions, nor is he looking for quick profits. He says himself that he might have grown rich much more quickly by other methods, but he did not choose to employ them. He might equally, and this also he says or implies, have crashed into spectacular ruin.

2nd August, 1982. Frederick Bandet hands over a donation by Hunting Gate to the Appeal for The Queen Elizabeth The Queen Mother Theatre, a new theatre in Woodside, Hitchin.
Left to Right: Richard Whitmore, BBC; Frederick Bandet; Jimmy Hill, ex-chairman of the Hertfordshire County Council; Eric Howlett.

Her Majesty Queen Elizabeth The Queen Mother at the opening of the new theatre at Woodside, Hitchin, 9th July, 1983.
Left to right: Frederick, Isabel, Henry and Gina Bandet.

The whole style of the man is quiet, not spectacular – no Aston Martin for him – and his manner, reserved, not extroverted, conveys a hint of melancholy, perhaps of loneliness. All this hardly sounds like a recipe for success in business, yet Frederick Bandet is an outstandingly successful business man.

Why?

Underlying all is a steely strength of purpose, founded on courage, which began to emerge when, as a lonely young foreigner in wartime England, he did not go to pieces as many – perhaps most – of us would have done. Instead, with a knack he has for turning adversity to advantage, he made a shrewd assessment of his position and resources, put some of his funds into leather, and went to the LCC's evening classes to learn how to put the leather to use. Then he saw an opportunity in Baldock – *Baldock*, of all places! – seized it, and within a year or so was self-supporting. What effort it must have cost him, anxious and lonely, thus to concentrate his energies and his resources, he does not say. Perhaps he does not care to remember.

After Frederick Bandet went into building, his strength of purpose remained, directed towards investment in property, and a far brighter prospect opened before him, because he thoroughly enjoyed what he was doing. The creative force of his personality began to flower. 'As soon as I began building', he says, 'I had seen a new world. I just enjoyed it'. Thus fortified, he began to develop his talent for financial management and for picking people.

In arranging his finances, his principle has always been to remain well within the range of his resources, both of cash and credit, never expanding his activities until he could see exactly what financial basis the expansion would rest on. For many years that meant slow progress, but he was content with that –

Offices and factory for Motorola at Stotfold, 1974.

it suited the cautious element in his nature – and he had his reward when there was a financial earthquake in 1973 - 74. Hunting Gate stood while other businesses, more adventurously funded, toppled.

Picking people, for twenty years or so, did not present Frederick Bandet with a very large problem. Once he had found Albert Haley, for whom he was indebted to Anthony King, he ran his business until the mid-sixties on hardly more than the proverbial 'two men and a boy', except that there was no boy. From the mid-sixties onward, as the business grew, he set about looking for young men who were, at first, over-qualified for the work he gave them to do.

His attitude towards professional qualifications is complex and revealing. On the one hand, having come from a background in which professional training was highly regarded, and having been professionally trained himself, he has a great respect for the knowledge and skill represented by letters after a man's name. On the other hand, there is an aspect of professionalism which he does not find easy to accommodate, and that is independence.

His quarrel with the architect early in his career made him determined not to run into the same situation again, and when he began to engage professionally-qualified managers he engaged them body and soul, to give their undivided attention to the business, providing the services which the business required. For the expenditure of energy, effort and talent which he demanded Frederick Bandet was prepared to offer extremely generous rewards.

Bandet has a propensity for making long-lasting. long-distance telephone calls often at unconventional hours. It arises partly from his enthusiasm for his work – some might call it an addiction

27,000 sq. ft. offices and warehousing for Fyffes Group, at Borehamwood, 1980.

24,000 sq.ft. extension for S.U. Butec at Thame, 1978.

– partly from his dislike of regular office hours; partly, perhaps, from loneliness. He denies that he has ever forced a call on anyone in his leisure time, ringing only if he feels that he is ringing a fellow enthusiast and ringing off at once if he feels that the call is unwelcome. Nor, he says, does he demand attendance at the office at weekends or out of hours. Nevertheless, it is probably not coincidental that those who have risen high in the business have been ready listeners on the telephone and ready attenders at the office and elsewhere at times which many might resent.

Frederick Bandet, like most successful business men, is an autocrat. He regards the Hunting Gate business, as he has every right to do, as his creation over which he has unquestionable rights of ownership. It follows that in his view all who work for the Group, including the Directors, are his employees and he is very sensitive indeed to any challenge to his authority. This was the central issue in each of the two serious quarrels he has been embroiled in while he has been concerned with Hunting Gate – two serious quarrels only, in the better part of forty years. In each case, rightly or wrongly, Bandet sensed danger to the underlying purpose of his life's work – the security of himself and his family – and his reaction was fierce and decisive.

Throughout the business Frederick Bandet's policy has been and still is to pay well for work done, and at the top his generosity has been extreme – some would say, excessive – including amongst the benefits offered opportunities to take up shares in Hunting Gate Group. Whether this practice has been entirely to the benefit of Frederick Bandet is open to doubt. It may have generated resentment rather than gratitude, and it certainly contributed to the acrimony of the dispute in 1981 over the question of a public issue.

15,000 sq. ft. office & warehousing for Chubb Fire Security at Cambridge, 1980.

That dispute was a clear sign that Hunting Gate is approaching a critical point in its history; a point that is reached by virtually all businesses that grow beyond a certain size in the founder's lifetime. The most difficult test in Frederick Bandet's career may be approaching: how to relax his grip on what he has built up without losing what he has striven for. Now, like the founders of other businesses before him, he must face the penalty of his success – the problem of reconciling his ownership and control, his deep instinct to have and to hold, his care for his family's interest, with the development of strong, self-confident management.

Nothing, perhaps, would please Frederick Bandet more than to see his own children and the children of others in the business – both Desmond and Howlett have sons – making a career in Hunting Gate. It would repeat the pattern of his childhood, when the firm of Hilfstein & Landerer represented a family alliance. So far as Bandet's children are concerned, both Isabel, his second daughter, and Henry, his son, take a keen interest in Hunting Gate's affairs.

This, however, is difficult and delicate ground. Bandet would not wish to press the younger generation into the business against their inclination, as his own father was pressed into *his* father's business. Nor must there be any ground for suspicion, amongst the generality of the employees, that the bosses' children are being favoured beyond their deserts.

There is in fact no nepotism. To all who come into it Hunting Gate offers a career open to talent. Moreover, if the past record of the business is anything to go by, it will offer the chance to develop whatever abilities a newcomer may offer on joining or discover after he has joined. The material rewards of success – again, if the future follows the pattern of the past – are likely to be high.

Offices and warehousing for E.L.E. International (left) and Fasson UK, at Hemel Hempstead.

Previous spread: 17,400 sq. ft. of offices for Price Waterhouse & Co. international Chartered Accountants at Windsor, 1983.

50,000 sq.ft. Superstore and offices for Texas Homecare at Southend, 1979.

Bandet's achievement in building up Hunting Gate and the Investment Companies has been superb, and he has a great deal of emotional capital invested in them, as most great business men have in the enterprises which are their monuments before the world and before posterity. For Frederick Bandet the companies he has founded are symbolic of his triumph over adversity. They meet his deep need for security. They satisfy his creative urge. They have made him wealthy, and they have provided him with a family estate to be handed on unimpaired to his children.

The wealth which Hunting Gate creates is not for Bandet and his family alone, but for the community at large. Apart from the employment which the Group provides in its own activities, there is the wealth in various forms, widespread through society, which is represented by the factories, offices and houses which over the years have been brought into being where no such buildings stood before. This is the positive creative side of property development – not the mere snatching of quick profit from a rise in the market – and the places where '4444' has been seen on building sites, especially the town of Hitchin, are the richer for it.

Frederick Bandet built Hunting Gate with courage, perseverance, integrity, generosity – all the classic qualities of Smilesian* man, today perhaps more readily appreciated than they were a few years ago. The business is expanding on the foundations which he laid. Its management is energetic, ambitious, intent on growth. In the sombre uncertainties of the early eighties, few firms have more solid ground for confidence in the future.

*see Samuel Smiles : *Self-Help*, 1859

EPILOGUE

By Frederick Bandet

Epilogue

When the idea of this biography was first mentioned, I did not think it was a very good one. It seemed to me rather pretentious. What had I done to justify such a book? I had always kept a low profile; I was not some 'Captain of Industry' whose name was known to millions, nor did I think my life's work would be of any great interest to anybody else.

It was John Cowen who eventually persuaded me that the story of Hunting Gate *is* worth telling. It is a story of enterprise, not of mine alone but of many whose hard and dedicated work, at all levels, have made our Company the success it is today. This book, therefore, is more a tribute to them than it is to me.

As I read the first draft, I felt a little like the hiker who, approaching the top of a hill, pauses and turns round. He looks back down his path; he sees the stones and boulders that littered his way; the mists that obscured the route, and the landslide that swept part of it away. Having reached the top, some of those obstacles now appear less formidable than when they were encountered. He remembers, with affection and nostalgia, the people he met on the way.

As I reach the summit of my sixties, I do confess to feeling a sense of achievement. Together, my colleagues and I have experienced the rough as well as the smooth: the worst property collapse in living memory and a bad recession are among the landmarks. We have not just survived; we have created something good that has given employment to hundreds, possibly thousands of people in and beyond our own Company and we have done our fair share in creating wealth for the community at large.

Working with Dr Reader over the past year has not just been a trip down Memory Lane; it has given me the opportunity ('forced' might be a better description!) not only to look up from my desk but also to get up from it, and away from the array of papers that seem perpetually to cover it, and think about the things that really matter in life.

I do not admit to old age–as Lord Samuel, I believe, once said, it is always 10 years away!–but I have not reached my present age without knowing how important it is to enjoy and take pleasure from the present. Since most of us spend a large part of our lives working and the remainder, hopefully, enjoying its fruits, that means enjoying our work, making close and lasting relationships with our colleagues and, very important, spending the time doing something worthwhile.

I particularly value the close, personal relationships I have been fortunate to form over the past fifteen years or so. From where I stand, the Home Counties and California are not so far apart. Today's advanced technology (by which I mean modern communications gadgets of which I am inordinately fond!) bring such distant parts, in fact, very near. This makes it especially tempting, on occasion, to become more involved in the affairs of the Company than good sense permits; it is called interference and is a temptation that confronts most founders–and parents–from time to time! My role nowadays, however, is that of a shareholder and in that role I do now and intend always to keep in close touch with businesses that continue to engage my daily interest, and with the people who run them, whom I like and admire. I have tried to give good advice when I am asked for it and the Management will be happy to tell anyone who will listen that this invariably includes strong financial control, cautious accounting and valuation policies, and avoiding all offers of funny money!

So far as doing something worthwhile is concerned, I believe Hunting Gate is a good Company, a happy Company, a Company that adds to our national stock not only through bricks and mortar, but also in terms of the employment and well-being of people. It is a Company in which the Old Guard has made room for younger, able executives, in all positions throughout the Group, and has given them the confidence and the authority to carry on the work they started. I believe this is true and I do, therefore, believe passionately that what I have worked for has indeed been worthwhile.

What of the future? I have a sense of optimism for the outlook. The foundations of our Company are strong. We are not afraid of seeking out and employing the very best people we can find to fill each and every position, and well balanced leadership will help us to progress into the next century. We will remain private, and continue to enjoy the many benefits of not being a public company, so long as my family and I judge that this is in the best interest of *everyone*, owners and employees alike. It allows me to say, with confidence, that the sons and daughters of my present colleagues–and of those yet to come–will be welcome if they decide to join their fathers, or their mothers for that matter. We are still small enough to have a long way to go, on two continents, and if they take the same pride, and work as well and as hard as their parents did, they too will enjoy satisfying and successful careers always, I hope, without the fear of waking up one morning to find they have been 'taken over' and made redundant. That is partly why I blocked the proposal to 'go public' in 1981.

Most of all I feel optimistic for the future of mankind itself. As I write, the question of unilateral versus multi-lateral nuclear disarmament is being vigorously debated. I have lived through two World Wars; more than most, I have reason to abhor the results of such conflicts.

My optimism is based on this: during the Second World War, both sides were ready for poison gas warfare. Similarly, so long as the West remains prepared, I do not believe a nuclear war will happen. Mankind will, doubtless, struggle through numerous ethnic and social crises but, simultaneously, advances in science will improve the environment and extend our lives. If the few who are able to create wealth are allowed and encouraged to do so, and they share it equitably, it will advance the prospect of greater understanding between nations and better, happier relationships between individuals.

I would like to thank the Directors of Hunting Gate for commissioning this book. It is an honour that I happily share with all those for whom the story of how Hunting Gate started and prospered is also part of their own lives.

I also want to thank Dr Reader for all his hard work delving into corners and memories on both sides of the Atlantic. In parts he exposed 'warts and all', details that I might have preferred to have been glossed over; in other parts, he might have given me more credit than I consider I deserve. Although it was not possible for Dr Reader to encompass all the very many people who have been, and still are helpful to me, he certainly met and talked to a great number and I am grateful that they gave so willingly and generously of their time. To those who are not mentioned, I would especially like to say that I do think of you with appreciation and good feelings.

To all who climbed the hill with me, the warmest 'thank you' of all. I did not, and could not have done it alone. I hope you enjoyed it as much as I did; I hope it was fun as well as hard work. I hope you feel, as I feel, that Hunting Gate is an enlargement of your own family as it is of mine and that, if we have done nothing else, we have at least started something that will be as good for the generations that come after us as it was for us.

June, 1983 FB
California

The success
of Hunting Gate
is based on the people
it has employed;
these are some of those people

Directors of Hunting Gate Developments.
Left to right: K.W. Grundy, R.D. Maxted, J.P. Walters, S.W. Holloway.
Inset M. McPherson.

Directors of Hunting Gate Construction. Left to right:
D. Mathews, M. D. Hemmings, Managing Director, D. Jump.

Directors of Hunting Gate Homes.
Left to right: M. Collins, J.T. Mills, K.C. Price, Managing Director D. Wilson, J.G. Hughes.

Michael Rickards,
Managing Director, Hunting Gate Property Services.

Anthony Ball
Land Surveyor to Hunting Gate Developments.

Keith Bygraves
Site Agent for Hunting Gate Construction.

Angus Docherty
Maintenance Manager, Hunting Gate Homes.

Linda Fletcher
Quantity Surveyor to Hunting Gate Developments.

Pat Grizzell with Mrs. Gladys Backurst – long serving members of the Accounts Department with 25 years' service between them.

Julia Harvey, Receptionist at Hunting Gate head office, with Peter Smyth

Fred Hillyard
Joiner, Hunting Gate Construction.

William Hodges
Site Agent for Hunting Gate Homes.

Mike Keen
Legal Executive to Hunting Gate Developments.

Fred Pateman
Site Agent for Hunting Gate Construction.

George Poyser
Site Agent for Hunting Gate Construction.

Peter Sanctuary, Director of Graphics Services
with one of his design staff, Freda Warrington.

Stan Sawyer
Southern Area Manager Hunting Gate Construction.

Kevin Tyler
Materials Buyer, Hunting Gate Construction.

John Washington
Planning Consultant to Hunting Gate Group

Pauline Woods
Secretary to D.F. Desmond, Managing Director, Hunting Gate Group.

Appendix 1

INDUSTRIAL & COMMERCIAL DEVELOPMENTS

Client	Location	Area sq. ft.	Type
Abbey National Pension Fund	High Street, Maidenhead	16,190	Offices
BICC Pension Fund	Orton-Southgate, Peterborough	10,000	Offices
BOC Group plc	Faraday Road, Swindon	54,110	Office/ Industrial
Boots Pensions Ltd.	Orton-Southgate, Peterborough	80,000	Industrial
	Lytton Way, Stevenage	50,000	Offices
British Airports Authority Superannuation Scheme	Hitchin Road, Henlow	20,000	Industrial
British Steel Pension Fund	High Street, Mitcham	34,500	Retail & Offices
Browne & Day Limited	Camford Way, Luton	35,000	Industrial
Clerical Medical & General Life Assurance Society	Great West Road Brentford	97,500	Industrial Office Refurbishment
Commercial Union Assurance	Sarum Hill Basingstoke	6,600	Offices
	High Street Crawley	22,750	Offices
	115 High Street, Crawley	11,820	Offices
	Oxford Street, Newbury	8,500	Offices
	18-20 Sheet Street, Windsor	5,800	Offices

Client	**Location**	**Area sq.ft.**	**Type**
Electricity Supply Nominees Limited	Cleveland Way, Hemel Hempstead	30,400	Industrial
Emmanuel College Cambridge	Farmyard, Windsor	7,810	Offices
Equitable Life Assurance Society	Rowley Lane, Borehamwood	99,000	Industrial
Fyffes Group Limited	Elstree Way, Borehamwood	26,950	Industrial
GTE Unistrut Limited	Edison Road, Bedford	23,630	Industrial
Hambro Life Property Fund Limited	Hudson Road, Bedford	51,870	Industrial
	Cleveland Road, Hemel Hempstead	40,000	Industrial & Offices
	Foundry Lane, Horsham	50,000	Industrial
	Humberstone Road, Leicester	34,500	Retail
	Dunhams Lane, Letchworth	75,000	Industrial
	Hythe Road, London	79,190	Industrial
	London Road, Southend	50,000	Retail
	Garman Road, Tottenham	100,000	Industrial
	Imperial Way, Watford	75,600	Industrial

Client	Location	Area sq.ft.	Type
Harris Queensway plc	Poynters Road, Luton	25,000	Retail & Flats
Hunting Gate Investments Limited	Foundry Lane, Horsham	43,120	Industrial
	Spur Road, Orpington	6,500	Offices
	Baldock Street, Royston	23,200	Retail
	Watchmead Welwyn Garden City	48,930	Industrial
ICI Pension Fund Securities Limited	Carlyle Road, Cambridge	13,450	Offices
John Lewis Partnership Pension Trust	Old Barn Lane, Kenly	54,000	Industrial
National Provident Institution	Church Street, West Woking	10,720	Offices
National Water Council	High Street, Aylesbury	3,630	Retail
Royal Insurance	South Park, Sevenoaks	25,000	Offices
Strathclyde Regional Council Pension Fund	Victoria Street, Windsor	20,635	Offices
United Builders Merchants Pension Fund	Winklebury Way, Basingstoke	18,000	Industrial
	London Road, Grays	13,150	Retail

Appendix 2

OCCUPIERS OF THE INDUSTRIAL ESTATES

HITCHIN

Dawnstoke Computer Services Ltd.
Dawnstoke Industrial Ltd.
Cornerhill Polythene Ltd.
International Computers Ltd.
R.S.T. Printers Ltd.
Everett Charles (U.K.) Ltd.
Drewton Beck Ltd.
Elmside Electronics Co. Ltd.
Plasmoulds Ltd.
Brown Boveri Kent plc
Lipha Pharmaceuticals Ltd.
Aydin Controls (U.K.) Ltd.
Kerry Ultrasonics Ltd.
F.J. Warren Ltd.
Freston Mould Products Ltd.
N.A.B. Precision Tooling Ltd.
Transworld Packaging Ltd.
McCorquodales Security Printers Ltd.
I.M.I. Yorkshire Imperial Ltd.
Institution of Electrical Engineers
Department of the Environment
Lightguards Ltd.
American Technical Publishers Ltd.
Microwave Systems Ltd.

WOOLMER GREEN
Electro Oil International Ltd.

BALDOCK
Panel Fabrications (Letchworth) Ltd.

ARLESEY
Rydelco Ltd.
Heatherside Engineering Ltd.
John Willmott Property Ltd.

WELWYN GARDEN CITY
Marconi Avionics Ltd.
Pattern & Marine Engineering Ltd.

STOTFOLD
Motorola Ltd.

HENLOW
Seary Phillips Ltd.
Spring Grove plc
Vent Duct Ltd.
F.D.R. Tools Ltd.
Finlim Plastics Ltd.
Intel Electronics Ltd.
Schlegel (U.K.) Engineering Ltd.
Texas Homecare
Henlow Sheet Metal Ltd.

HOUGHTON REGIS
H. McIntyre & Sons Ltd.
Luton Suspended Ceilings & Supplies Ltd.
Chiltern Precision Ltd.
Autocraft Ltd.
Teledyne Ltd.
Petters Refrigeration Ltd.

WATFORD
The General Electric Co. plc

BOREHAMWOOD
Fyffes Group Ltd.
Goodyear Tyre & Rubber Co. Great Britain Ltd.

BEDFORD
G.T.E. Unistrut Ltd.
The Boots Company plc
Terinex Ltd.
Saxon Body Works Ltd.
Striker Engineering Ltd.
Bedford Tool & Gauge
Windshields
Challenge Industrial Fastenings Ltd
Cycles Peugot (U.K.) Ltd.
Linfood Holdings plc
P.G.W. Holdings Ltd.

ANDOVER
Rowater Medical Ltd.
Space Models Ltd.
I.P.C. Magazines Ltd.
Express Parcel Services
Klargester Engineers Ltd.
Tri Seal Mouldings Ltd.
Southern Sanitary Specialists Ltd.
P.J. Holloway Sales Ltd.
Eraser International Ltd.
Longfield Instruments Ltd.
Texicoat Ltd.
M.J.S. Glassworks Ltd.

THAME
Neweld Plastics (U.K.) Ltd.
Antiference Ltd.
Cheverton & Laidler Ltd.
Frank Odell Ltd.
Thame Systems Ltd.
Austin Rover Group Ltd.
Sprecher & Schuh U.K. Ltd.

CARTERTON
Meath Engineering (Tools) Ltd.
Nelson & Co. (Ashford) Ltd.
Johnstone Safety Ltd.
R.J. Cox Precision Engineers Ltd.

ORPINGTON
Watkins Gray International (U.K.)

Appendix 3

HUNTING GATE GROUP: EIGHT YEAR FINANCIAL SUMMARY

	1975	1976	1977	1978	1979	1980	1981	1982
Turnover (£000's)	1,436	2,390	4,675	7,328	10,739	18,134	30,558	31,841
Profit before exceptional items (£000's)	166	178	398	591	937	948	1,609	1,900
Earnings per share	33p	18p	40p	59p	94p	90p	157p	173p
Investment properties (£000's)	8	8	359	692	2,116	2,828	5,137	7,711
Shareholder's funds (£000's)	13	235	633	1,479	3,066	4,250	6,044	8,590

Index

The following abbreviations have been used—FB for Frederick Bandet and HG for Hunting Gate. The page numbers of illustrations are printed in italics (*44*).

Index

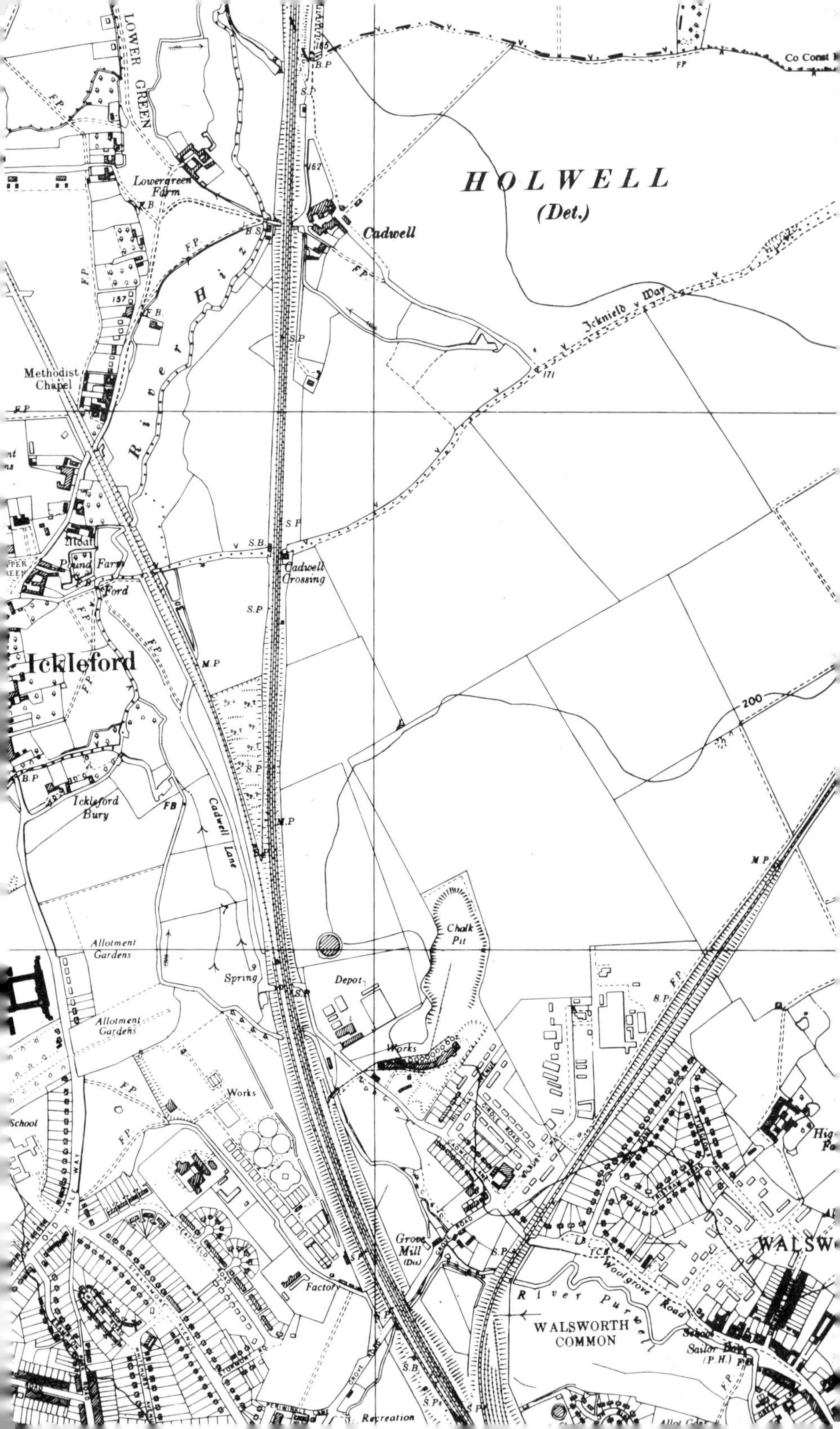

LOWER GREEN
Lowergreen Farm
HOLWELL
(Det.)
Cadwell
Icknield Way
River Hiz
Methodist Chapel
Pound Farm
Ford
Cadwell Crossing
Ickleford
Ickleford Bury
Cadwell Lane
Allotment Gardens
Spring
Depot
Chalk Pit
Works
School
Factory
Grove Mill (Dis)
River Purwell
WALSWORTH COMMON
Woolgrove Road
Sailor Boy (P.H.)
Recreation
Co Const
200